T0195692

Letters to a Friend
Sharing Thoughts and Experiences

BOB APEL

WESTBOW
PRESS®
A DIVISION OF THOMAS NELSON
& ZONDERVAN

WestBow Press books may be ordered through
booksellers or by contacting:

WestBow Press
A Division of Thomas Nelson & Zondervan
1663 Liberty Drive
Bloomington, IN 47403
www.westbowpress.com
844-714-3454

Scripture quotations taken from The Holy Bible, New International
Version® NIV® Copyright © 1973 1978 1984 2011 by Biblica,
Inc. TM. Used by permission. All rights reserved worldwide.

ISBN: 978-1-6642-7694-9 (sc)
ISBN: 978-1-6642-7695-6 (hc)
ISBN: 978-1-6642-7693-2 (e)

Library of Congress Control Number: 2022916158

Print information available on the last page.

WestBow Press rev. date: 09/01/2022

Dedicated to anyone who has suffered
under modern-day Pharisees.

Contents

Why Call You Friend?

A sharing of thoughts and experience

Zip 121

Apel
Average Guy
Zip 121

Dear Friend,

Why Call You Friend?

This is the first question, and the answer is simple—because friends is what we are. We have many years of history. We have worked and shared life together. Friends are sought-after assets that add to the quality of life. They are characterized by offering acceptance as is, without conditions. They share common experiences so both may obtain a clearer understanding of life's journey. No two are alike, so the differing points of view add to our own decision-making processes.

These letters are written to fill a void in my heart for your journey. Time and your willingness to share have exposed how other people have hurt you with misguided pressure when it comes to faith and belief. Today, early positive thoughts about faith are discarded for nonbelief. I understand and respect what you have endured. Having a different experience and view, I ache to share a positive view and results. I have tried discussions until you asked me to stop. I see no value in exposing you to something you neither want nor can see any possible benefit from. This leaves only one avenue, which I have determined to be letters to be read on your own, in your own space and time. This effort is not to persuade you to think as I do but rather to help you consider or reconsider the results of things that have been done to you. These letters are the only offering I have to help heal the past, of which I was not a part.

You are a friend because we share more in common than not. Neither of us asked to be born. We had no say in when, where, or by which parents. As infants, our needs were feeding, changing, and sleeping. How those needs were met influenced the people we were becoming. Psychologists tell us much of our character is determined by the age of five; as a result, some may have or lack patience. Character building begins without much of our input. Maturity becomes an adjustment of previously set factors.

On the other end of the journey, we all know we are going to die. Again, excluding suicide, we have no say in when, where, or how. The possibilities range from sudden and painless to prolonged and painful and anywhere in between. Most of us hope for the easier route. People mistakenly believe they are in control of death if they do it themselves. It is true only for them, but suicide is one of the most hurtful acts they can thrust on another. The question remains, were they really in control of death, or was that an illusion? The punishment for others lasts a lifetime.

In the time between birth and death, we share common experiences in the struggle around life's questions. We have a thirst and need to figure out who we are. Contained in that quest is an understanding of childhood influence, where we are now, and what we can change.

The second question is what is our purpose? There seems to be a built-in need to have or be of some relevance. Do you have a place to make a difference in society or even a small area? As humans, we have different reactions. One group denies the questions exist and ignores them. Others know their importance but shrink in fear. Others accept the challenge but become overwhelmed by worry and are sure they will get it wrong.

Yet there are people who see an opportunity to test answers and make their own choices. In the end, they find fruitful answers. In my experience, these questions remain fluid. Some steps must be taken in one direction to discover there is more meaning in another. Further, these missteps prepare us and give us confidence in the new direction. This is the start of sharing an individual story—mine.

While these letters are intended for you, I see the possibility that others may have been subjected to similar abuse. Sometimes people are misguided. The bottom line, however, is they are starved for control to create their image of self-worth. For me, it is painful to watch, as it robs every one of their abilities to make choices. Therefore, please understand we are not alone. Others may read these letters not for judgment but as measures of their own choices or ability to make them. My hope is some benefit will come of your reading these letters. Choice is a cornerstone of life not to be lost.

Please understand a few basic things about me and the purpose of these letters. I represent average intelligence and experience. Understand, there are smarter, better educated, and more persuasive people ready, willing, and able to dismantle all these thoughts. That is fine in their place. This effort is to offer you another point of view for your consideration. These letters are not in competition with others. I only wish to explain what I was thinking, what decisions were made, and the results, nothing more. Also, I'm average because there is nothing special about me. I had no unusual background or upbringing.

I have not risen to a notable place that would offer me any special consideration. This assessment is not self-deprecating but rather a sober reality of the impact I have had. I will explain this in future letters. Being average also allows us to relate to one another's experiences. You, I, and most who read these letters are average. There is a hidden treasure in being average. I believe that position offers more balance in thinking, opportunity, and outcome. I personally see average as an asset, not a liability, in a world that garners extremes and social division. Balance can be an antidote and a useful friend. We are in this together, and the letters are a way for me to fulfill my purpose.

The third question is what are we to do? The world gets us to focus on this question all the time. It is considered without ever thinking about who we are, or why we are here. What a tragedy.

The fourth, and overarching, question that influences the first three needs recognition: simply, is there a Creator? How this is answered will have a significant impact on living out the who, why, and what. Being upfront, I am a theist (a person who believes in the existence of a god or gods, specifically a creator who intervenes in the universe). Given that and the concern of your previous pain at the hands of others, these letters are straightforward, simple, and lack emotionally charged jargon that stifles honest contemplation. The terms will be limited to things I believe will point in a direction but not inflame. Words like *Creator, theist,* and *atheist* connote the topic but little else. These seem acceptable ways to group thought without advocating one or the other. I hope you agree. If by chance an old word triggers pain, please know that is not the intent. I therefore ask for forgiveness in advance. If it is any consolation, the people of "faith" who have hurt you have been roundly criticized in the accepted Word of the Creator. Further, the beliefs and experiences are backed up by a long history of study and living examples. Since those are not a part of this effort, I have included those in a separate section at the end of the letters. Please consider this as an option if you desire to understand the motivation and thoughts that have guided me to this point. If the letters have not roused any desire, please just ignore them. It is, however, a more important section because that is where true guidance is found. I can only suggest and testify, but there is real transformation and life waiting for you to consider and accept. I am not able to give those to you. A greater being can if you are open. The references listed have inspired my journey. I believe the ones listed and others that will show up in time will offer equal or greater returns. Personal growth, a feeling of belonging, self-worth, and living your purpose can be the ultimate rewards. These letters are not to condemn but to encourage you to have these gifts.

As these letters unfold, I will point out recurring themes over and over again. Therefore, I will reference *four code words* to explain the thoughts in each situation.

- The first is *control*. Who is trying to control who and for what purpose?
- The second that is always tied to control is *rejection*. Who or what is standing in the way of control that requires rejection? In my mind, these

come down to the two most critical forces in any thought or discussion.

The antidote for these negative forces is in the next two code words.

- The first positive is *believe* or *belief*. Whatever guides your discernment process helps determine your result.
- The next is *trust*. What outside yourself is there to trust when making a decision? Most decisions for me come down to a competition between these forces. Therefore, have these words in mind with this understanding.

Another recurring theme is *parlor tricks*. These are one or two words added to a discussion that are designed to limit the proof required to make a point. Further, they have the unfortunate ability to denigrate the person holding a different view. An example is referring to theist beliefs as fairy tales. This label limits validity and dismisses the believer as a child. Time has taught me to look for and understand how parlor tricks are used to control thoughts and other people. Understanding their existence has offered me clarity on many occasions.

Next, the term *analogy* has become a staple to my thought process over time. Understanding a complex idea in relation to a similar simple concept has offered me some level of confidence in resolution. As I've grown older, experience has taught me to seek this form of clarity. Today, I just think like that in most cases. The concept does not always work, especially for other people. I only claim it helps me. It is offered to you as another consideration.

The last theme is that of the two governing forces of *fear versus love*. Fear is the negative, and love is the antidote. I have recently come to understand there are five types of fear.

1. The most common is fear of death. We all eventually come to understand the certainty of dying. We also understand the various ways that happens. So, we live with thoughts of how and when. Young people feel invincible and it is less a focus. As we age, the thoughts become more prevalent and disconcerting.
2. Another fear is that of attack. With societal division and unrest, being physically and emotionally attacked has become a common expectation.
3. Next would be the fear of lack of control. Wanting to be in control is foremost in each mind in one way or another. Loss of control can be very debilitating.
4. We also fear not being relevant or having a purpose. Life without any purpose can become depressing. We can handle conflict if we believe there is a better reason. Without purpose, life can become awfully long and frustrating.
5. Lastly is fear of the future. Not knowing what is going to happen can freeze us in an untenable position.

These fears can be such invasive forces that they end up dictating decisions and actions we later wish we could do over. From experience, when able to bring genuine concern for others, these negative forces seem to be held at bay. Giving to others freely is an act of love. Given without strings, or expectations, this love can be of benefit to others in their choices. Thus, in many circumstances, love has overcome potentially destructive behavior. When appropriate, decisions that have that affect can be discussed.

As a tool for these letters, there will be suggested topics or questions based on the content at the end of each letter. You have a right to your own thoughts and understandings. Some of the topics have long-standing possibilities and consequences. These only represent a sharing from my journey. Not necessarily right or wrong, just fodder for thought.

The topics for the letters is on

- Creator
- Who am I?
- Why am I here?
- What am I to do?
- Men and women
- Leadership
- Discipline
- Direction
- Pain
- Value of life
- Right and wrong
- Disunity, and
- Finishing strong.

It is my hope you can make your way through this attempt to share.

Suggestions for consideration:

Would having another point of view from a friend be helpful in your journey?

Does the format make sense, and is it an acceptable form?

Creator - Yes or No?

A sharing of thoughts and experience

Zip 121

Apel

Average Guy

Zip 121

Dear Friend,

Creator—Yes or No

It is a simple question but difficult to answer. This letter will only discuss conclusions that have developed over years of thinking, reading, and personal experience. Emotions, both positive and negative, can divide thoughtful communication. As stated previously, using charged words can only create barriers.

This subject is crowded with intellectuals and apologists on both sides of the question. I make no pretense of being either. I have summarized Bible passages that have influenced my beliefs in the section marked the Supporting Word from God (the final chapter in this book). This is included if interest is stirred and you desire more understanding. If there is no interest, please skip those words.

Since part of my who is to I think differently than most people, I offer three simple considerations.

- First, if one had the ability to be a Creator, how and why would you do it?
- Second, would you not include specific clues that anyone, at any time, and anywhere would have the ability to understand that there was a Creator or at least intelligent design?
- Third, would you not include relationships with animals and other parts of creation to reinforce the intent of what we experience?

What would it take to create the universe? The definition I have come to understand would be someone outside time, space, and matter. You would need to exist before the start. This is the beginning of doubt since we have no experience or reference to these qualities or abilities. Further, having such power would also include a value system other than any we have experienced. This would include accepting what we would consider harm if there was an ultimate offsetting good. You would want the best for each part and offer care to see that happen. Also, you would want this to occur in relationship by mutual consent, not forced.

The work would start with a full spectrum of opportunities and experiences. These would include colors, textures, sky, moon, stars, water, plants, mountains, plains, and deserts. As a crowning touch you might add a partner to manage the rest. The key piece would be a dynamic relationship with all.

I have an analogy that helps consider why choice to participate was an essential element. I grew up loving model trains and enjoyed making realistic layouts. No matter how sophisticated, the designs always violated speed, turning radius, and grade change that are musts for real trains.

In the end, the excitement was in creating, not the operating. When complete, the setup became less interesting. Therefore, in setting up creation, and wanting a dynamic relationship, there would be two alternatives, either forced into it or given the choice to opt out of it. If we were forced, we would be no more than mindless robots. That approach would appear useless and even boring. I would think a Creator would want to be engaged in every aspect, but not in a forced way. Would you make that a part of your creation? The way would be to offer a relationship based on belief and trust. You would obviously care about the creation, as you put all your time, talent, and treasure into it. Given your understanding, you would also know there would be rejection instead of acceptance. The point is that fore knowledge and predetermination are not the same. Knowing human response does not mean force needs to be used to obtain the desired result. Therefore, existence that is led to the fullest would include the offer of reconciliation, forgiveness, grace, hope, and guidance. The creation would be offered all these attributes available in overflowing abundance to allow creation to unfold as intended. Having predetermination would preclude choice.

Often in our interactions with the Creator, we demand proof to believe. The problem with that arrogant approach is the Creator is not subject to our "acceptable proof." If proof were given, then choice would automatically be removed. Humans cannot have it both ways. Either there is control, and rejection, or freewill based on belief and trust. Isn't it logical to give us free choice, even knowing the result?

This seems to be centered on a redeeming personal dynamic relationship. While I understand more complex mathematical forms of logic, I go back to A implies B, B implies C, therefore A implies C. I am not able to make sense out of a predetermined creation but can wrap my head around an evolving dynamic relationship. Having love and concern would also mean following planning and setup of daily interactions of eight billion people. Given the skills needed to create, giving daily personal interactions with others, and weaving them into benefit for each would not seem too big a task. This would work knowing our hearts, needs, and potential outcomes. Since all is subject to having choice, belief and trust are the ingredients to give each person their most fruitful evolving steps.

Another less-considered thought, even ignored, is the daily proof of existence that surrounds us every day. This could be considered the Creator's fingerprints. In my mind, it is a huge stretch to believe rocks, trees, fields, brooks, lakes, mountains, deserts, and skies are all accidental evolution of the fittest. Have you ever witnessed order coming out of chaos? Would anyone expect to pour out red, white, and blue confetti from a second-story balcony and believe it would form an American flag on the ground? Animals and humans are far more complex than flags. With all the clamor of intellectual discussion on the existence of a Creator, and demanded proof, isn't a wonder that doubt goes on with the proof all around us? Certainly, a Creator would make a relationship commitment the highest expectation for humans and himself. Why do we ask for what we already have? Why do we not accept responsibility for having what is needed to join in the relationship? Why do we resist? The simple answer is wanting to be in control and a determination to reject the one they should seek. We want to control everything, but that is not our role or one that we are qualified to exercise. Why do we think like that? It would seem to be our human nature. It is a reality, but not the design. These are thoughts worth considering.

What about those who have never heard of the

Creator or the plan? No one would seem to be exempt given all the natural cues. Also given the development of instant worldwide communications, Internet, and travel, the totally shutout are a dwindling few. Creation cues are often ignored in favor of arguments that can be won or lost. No matter who you are or what your experience has been, the question remains: yes or no?

As I consider my own experiences, childbirth becomes one of awe and amazement. For me it is more confirmation of an engaged Creator. In our family, we committed to my being in the delivery room even before conception. Being a male and offering the only support I could, it was a natural decision. It was a relatively new option at the time. We were the doctor's first try, even though he was close to retirement. I have had that experience with all three of our children and once with a grandson. Seeing that first look and breath of new life remains inspiring. Knowing you in some small part were an enabling factor brings a new connection to all of creation. It is a first step in engaging your purpose. Creation would continue another day because you filled a role planned long ago. The completion of one small act brings a completeness that the world has yet to offer. In my life, partaking in this event and the journey of children only cemented my commitment, belief, and trust. How could it not?

The last consideration is the relationship we have been given with animals. In my case, I have had connection with nine dogs and three cats. The dogs are my closest connections, with there being eight different breeds. Each one was different but special in his own way. They were young and old, big and small, fast and slow, hyper and not, barkers and quiet. Each came into my life at an appropriate time with tools to meet my situation. The relationships are so notable because verbal interaction is limited. It is a reminder that most communication is nonverbal. Dogs learn a few words but do not speak. Yet, through getting to know each other, both understand each other's moods and needs.

Our current dog reads like an open book by just looking into her eyes, and vice versa. Being greeted to the door each night is the start of knowing. She lets me know she cares about how I feel. She also wants me to know it is mealtime. We have many routines during the day. There is the expected, even demanded banana each morning. At certain times, there are expected walks or times outside. Overall, the usual need for control and rejection are missing. This pattern if applied to our human relations might have ever lasting effects. Creation might take on a look that was originally intended. With experiences, emotions, and meaningful results, it makes it harder for me to conceive of a world without intelligent design.

Since we looked at these simple ideas, I am encouraged to believe. There are ways we all are challenged. For simplicity, there is theism and atheism. The question is yes or no. Maybe comes out as agnostic. There seems to be groups in that category. Ones that say they do not believe but are open. The other ones do not believe and use agnostic as a socially acceptable way of saying no. In my experience most agnostics just do not want negative feelings for being honest and saying no. These letters are intended for those still open. There is no expectation of changing those that do not want to consider or reconsider. I am not able to convince anyone of anything. I can only offer perspective to another. Even if I could be of influence, a dynamic relationship can only exist if it is wanted.

The question of existence is not a one-and-done proposition. It cannot be a once-thought-through event, settled and finished. Most want it that way, but unfortunately, it is not. The challenges are daily and require a renewed commitment. This continued process is not easy. I can only attest that it becomes like breathing. When I am open to my limitations, the Creator can do the heavy lifting of helping me understand a meaningful part in creation.

Both theism and atheism are belief systems. At the risk of an emotionally charged word, both hinge on faith. I define faith as belief in something not proven. This applies to both groups equally. Often, I am confronted with, "But science has proven there is no Creator." This is an amazing statement when you consider the definition of science. If it is accepted as systematic knowledge of the physical or material world gained through observation and experimentation, then we are left with the question of it being discovered or revealed. Think of all the passionate people that had this discussion on the world being flat. At that point it was not proven. Many lived in fear believing it was true. Their conviction, however sincere, did not make it true. Their lives were negatively impacted because the truth had not been revealed. This analogy could apply to both theism and atheism. Both are relying on determining the value of what has been reveled not discovered. Revelation goes beyond discovery. The question becomes could creation use the knowledge before that time? Was it ready to accept and use the knowledge? I would submit creation is a work in progress, which is a controlled unfolding. The round world was always a reality, just not proven. It was revealed, which helped relieve misguided fears.

Continuing the same thoughts today of our understanding of DNA: Has DNA always existed? Did we invent it or was it revealed? DNA, in my understanding, has always existed. It explains much of human development that we have never understood. Are each one really as different as people? Does DNA hold the keys to unlocking solutions to physical and medical problems? I believe the answer is yes to all. As a side issue, what are we going to say if we find two DNAs exactly alike? We now use this revealed information to convict and free persons charged with crimes. Previously, we had to rely on fingerprints, which are there but must be revealed with a powder. I suppose that history is part of attraction to the Creator's fingerprints as I see them. The point is DNA comes at a time in development where man can use the knowledge to either creatively solve issues or by choice add to his ability to control. Once again, we see control and rejection versus belief and trust. So many long for solutions and implore their pursuit, only to question the validity and source of the revealed knowledge. Bottom line: humans did not create DNA and all its possibilities; it was only given to them. Back to my amazement, I find it interesting that if science has proven there is no Creator beyond a doubt, how is it so many scientists, from all over the world, reach the exact opposite conclusion, and believe in a Creator, based on the same data? The question becomes which interpretation do you believe? Thus, both theism and atheism are belief-based systems.

Another challenge has been, "Belief is just a fairy tale." This is my favorite parlor trick. Let us dissect it. This basically dismisses the idea of belief as "obviously" unproven, intellectually starved belief of a child. This not only dismisses any validity in the discussion and conclusions, it demands acceptance with little or no proof. It's like the best defense is a good offense. Fairy tale not only devalues the discussion, it demeans the value of the person. It is a judgmental indictment by labeling one as an immature child. Fairytales are considered obvious untrue stories made up as a crutch for living this life. *Crutch* is another parlor trick. This label is an aid to the physically/mentally disabled. In this instance it becomes a demeaning characterization, used to win arguments but not requiring proof. Funny thing is I do not relate to seeing faith as a crutch. In my experience, it has enabled a new meaning for life. Every day I find new meaning, joy, and peace. It is evolving and never complete. This lends a new optimism about what the future holds.

The last challenge is the word *naïve*. It has many meanings, mostly negative. In my thinking, it is having or showing a lack of experience, judgment, or information. One could also include having an unaffected simplicity of nature or absence of artificiality; unsophisticated; ingenuous. The negative includes lack of experience, but isn't that the heart of scientific study? If we knew, we would not need study. I have a long history of lacking judgement and being considered naive. I tend to trust everyone until given a reason not to.

I have a funny life experience to make my point. As an architect, I had many interviews with potential clients to see if we had the chemistry to work to solve their needs.

I remember one interview like it was yesterday and have never forgotten its impact. Five minutes into the small talk, he said he needed to cut to the chase. He said was a manipulative jerk. Not thinking in a knee-jerk response, I said he was five minutes late in that admission. What should have been an insult became a badge of honor to him that he could be recognized as a dominating figure. We never did come to an ability to work together. I trusted him up to the time he made it apparent that I could not.

The point of this story goes deeper. I was not condemning him or his values. I was willing to accept him without reservation if I could provide a positive outcome in his life. What history had taught and the reason for not continuing was the fact that at some point the dominating nature would require me to do the wrong thing for the wrong reason. As inept as I am, a reasonable goal has been to do the right thing for the right reason. My goal is for a better track record. He ultimately was not open to finding the best solution, only what would serve himself. So, you see the rejection was not of him but rather avoiding stress in future confrontations for both of us. Further, it makes my case for being naïve.

This world is more divided today than what we have witnessed in the last hundred years. Maybe only the pandemic can return some form of unity. In this division are heard cries of "social justice." I would offer the thought that justice is more likely to occur by people open to trusting until given a reason not to. Being willing to accept people as they are and being committed to finding a positive outcome for them is the start of finding fairness. The world is founded on control and rejection, which is the basis for injustice. Being open to others' needs seems to be the way it was always intended to be. In my world, this is the heart for the dynamic relationship the Creator seeks but does not demand.

The last word in the thoughts of naïve was ingenuous. If that word means free from reserve, restraint, or dissimulation, candid, sincere, the question becomes are those negative attributes? To finish in this divided world, being naïve is not only shunned, it may also someday be illegal. My personal hope is when and if that happens, there is enough evidence to convict me.

So where does this discussion leave us? Offered are three simple reasons to consider belief and three challenges. There are libraries full of these discussions. This is only one more for your consideration.

Suggestions for consideration:

Are you beyond being open? Is it permanently fixed in your heart? If you were open, would you consider letting the Creator do the heavy lifting?

Apel
Average Guy
Zip 121

Who-Am I?

A sharing of thoughts and experience
Zip 121

Dear Friend,

Who Am I?

This subject is not widely considered when needed. In my case, it came as reflection after questionable choices. There is that word—choice—again. It seems to be a fulcrum around life. Who we are, in my mind, is the first question to consider after deciding if a Creator exists, since that view influences not only who we are but what our purpose is and what to do.

The who is initially determined by influences while growing up—from parents, family, society, and our environment—and natural abilities and liabilities, which came from heredity.

As for my experience, we were an average family of the 1940s, '50s, and '60s. Average is a word the world has taught us to reject. It connotes less than maximum performance, which is discouraged. Especially in America, where the work ethic is the dominate force. I received a strong one, but it has not always served me well. Funny, average is what most of us are. In reflection, I have come to embrace the word with a new sense of balance, not falling prey to extremes. Above average struggle with ego and manipulation. Below average struggle with self-worth and doubt. The interesting part is the three levels are closer than the world would let you believe. The smart ones are not that much smarter, and the lessor is just as smart but not permitted to believe it. Average has much to be desired and not ashamed.

An example of these thoughts was found on a mission trip to Honduras. It is an interesting culture, totally different from the states. From first exposure it was clear most people suffered from intestinal worms due to lack of clean water. Good wells were lost in an earthquake. We determined a solution would be to collect fresh water and pipe it to the village, about a two-mile run. The Americans would supply the technology, pipe, and filters. The locals would supply the labor. Being part of a mission trip, our local contacts, in this case, ended up being believers.

Now I want to introduce you to Carlos. He was the main local contact. He helped with all the preliminary work needed for approvals from the Honduran government. It took a year of weekly meetings to convince everyone of the sincerity of all involved, and what was proposed could happen. This country is accustomed to easy talk and no performance. Carlos walked six hours each way to these meetings in town. He gave up a whole day of work once a week for a year. Understand what that means. He worked his own land or hired out for three dollars a day. He and his family existed in a different economy on $700 dollars a year. So you see, giving up a day a week is a big commitment.

What was his motivation? He had lost a five-year old son to a waterborne disease. The most significant part of his effort, which we learned at the completion, was he did this knowing his family could not receive the clean water. His house was too far up the hill to be served. His belief system led him to do the right thing for the right reason. Currently, the community is trying to help build a new house within the accessible area in appreciation of his efforts. That would be a just reward, but note it was not the motivation.

Carlos is a rare man. Physically, he can work any of us under the table, any day, anywhere, at about five-foot, three-inches tall. He is humble. His trust will ultimately be rewarded. Decisions are not made on expectations. His needs will be met. In our part of the world, Carlos would be pitied, looked down upon, and considered less than average. I have a different take on him. As a friend and fellow worker, I would follow him and work with him anywhere for any project. It is a joy to be around him. How many Americans would dismiss him and cheat themselves out of a beautiful experience? Carlos knows who he is. How many average people here do we dismiss each day, and what are we both losing?

My own study of who I am starts with early childhood influences. My parents married in August 1929. They were what I refer to as "Depression parents" for obvious reasons. They did not even live together their first year. He dropped out of engineering school to work in a steel foundry to support his parents and brothers. She taught school in a farm community and lived with a family.

Personally, I developed bad eating habits, as I had to be a "clean plater." Much of those early requirements linger in my eating habits today. It was not all their fault, as I willingly enjoy food and even deceive myself into believing my habits are acceptable. Family influenced education as well. Elementary education was not as advanced as it is today. I have come to believe from later experiences that I had some form of attention deficit disorder. I have learned I do not take verbal commands completely. This came to light long after

I was a parent. Back in early school and at home I was thought to be dumb and lazy. That indictment would lead to becoming a workaholic. Work ethic and overcoming a poor image can have that affect. To compensate over the years, I have learned to revisit instructions and take more notes.

I had a similar educational adjustment in the first grade. We now know being right-handed or left-handed have other characteristics. Right-handed are believed to be more detail-oriented and decisive. Left-handed are more sensitive and creative. In the first grade, I wanted to be left-handed, but every day the pencil was moved to the right until I became right-handed. Left-handed was not an acceptable option. So you see, at some point this change had an influence on those other characteristics. This has its pluses and minuses. The creative may have developed differently, or the attention to detail developed more than it would have. It makes no difference today, but it is understandably a part of who I am. Therefore, no one needs to have blame or consider oneself odd. It just helps to understand how you got to be you. I do not feel bad or defensive, for the choice was not mine. It helps me understand some things I do or do not do, which is helpful. This kind of knowledge gives us peace and direction for the future.

Part of the future is understanding that who we are is always evolving. From a mediocre student through high school, there was a transition to a better student in college. I was motivated by the wonder and opportunities of becoming an architect. I could see even in the early days that this would be a lifelong journey that I would enjoy committing to everyday. To date, I have not been disappointed. Making my work feel as easy as breathing has been rewarding and even leading to a sense of purpose. Please do not misunderstand, the journey has not been easy or without stress. I think that is why we call it work. While not easy, there is sense of evolving toward who I am and who I was meant to be. What college failed to finish, the next phase in the service filled in needed voids. Like the army or not, it can offer challenges you have no choice to accept. Organization, accountability, performance, and public speaking are just a few of the avenues explored. I ended up believing the time on active duty was a million-dollar experience. I would not trade it or repeat it for a million dollars.

After service, I plunged into working on being a young husband and father, at the same time learning what college could not teach me about being an architect. This was truly a formative period. Without details, in forming who I am, I believe endurance and consistency came to the forefront. So much to do, and so little time to do, or as it seemed. Later life experiences would prove that to be a false concept. In reality, we only do what we want to do and make time for doing. The rest become excuses. Gaining understanding from experiences molds who we are.

The next adjustment to who I am came with a major part of lifetime work. I worked eleven years for an architectural firm and twenty years with a partner and other talented people. There were ups and downs all the time. I often worked too hard, but that was to cover the perception of being dumb and lazy. There are many issues to review, but one stands out. Early on, when we were in our own firm, we had to make a choice in how we served our clients. The practice was geared to a high volume of smaller projects. Budgets were often minimal and owner experience even less. We did land a few projects that offered more design challenge and budget. We won a couple of small awards—something to feel good about and talk to future clients about.

However, over time, it became apparent that that we could not serve two goals. Either we pushed for high-profile projects with name recognition, or we served the true needs of people who wanted guidance. At some point we turned our back on awards and focused on serving people who wanted our help. We were not there to tell others how to live. That was not our place. We were to offer choices our clients could understand. We placed an emphasis on balance in each project. The timing, budget, function, and creativity all had to have their proper place. What good is a creative structure if it does not serve the needs of the people using it? Strong form statements are great until they break the budget. The architectural community never understood us, valued us, or respected what we did or how we did it. I can only speak for myself, but serving became who I am.

The next adjustment came when I came to the end of myself. Working fifty-six hours a week for twenty years will do that. I will explain more of this in the "What Am I to Do?" letter. Other adjustments are still underway. Determining "Who Am I?" is a lifelong study for those engaged.

Suggestions for consideration:

Do you understand how parents, family, and others have influenced you? Do you see the discovery process as lifelong? Do you understand your gifts and abilities that make you unique?

Apel
Average Guy
Zip 121

Why Am I Here?

A sharing of thoughts and experience
Zip 121

Dear Friend,

Why Am I Here?

Does this question equate to purpose? Both theist and atheist seem to share a thirst for being relevant. Having purpose and being relevant is one of the five fears we all face. I am not sure I understand where the drive for this comes from for the atheist. It seems the desire to have an impact comes from wanting a civil, organized society for people to exist. Their time frame is birth, life, and then death. There is nothing else. There seems to be a value for society to improve. It is central to be a "good" person. That thought has two ways of manifesting itself.

There are atheists who have genuine concern for others and want the best for them. I am unclear on how that comes about, but I know it exists. There are others who, for appearance and control, want to portray being good. If they look that way, then we will like them, and they can have more influence with us.

Unfortunately, the same pattern befalls theists. Most theists I know have a concern for others. This, however, comes from a relationship with a Creator who cares for all equally. Left to our own devises, we are not capable of true concern for others. Theists have an understanding that no one is "truly good," not one. Only by acknowledging the Spirit of a Creator working in and through us can we project genuine love and respect for others. If we are honest, we have moments of appearing to provide for others, but down deep there is tension of control and rejection. Theists have the most impact when they come into alignment with the will of the Creator and who they were intended to be. Most of us come to not trust ourselves from our history. That is why we need to continually check our alignment and recommit to the one who has the power to offer a true transformation. This process leads to a truer understanding of purpose and how we can fit into the unfolding of creation.

Everyone has a different interest and need for making the "why I am here" connection. Many do not care and ignore the process. For some like myself, it becomes a reflection of past events that help to inform current decisions. What do I mean? When I was a child, thinking about why I am here was never on my radar. I thought like a child and acted like a child. The world did not have any expectation of my effectiveness. It was not a time to contribute but rather to listen and learn. As I grew, the measure of learning went from C in high school to B+ in college. After graduation, learning took another turn with two years in the army. Planning, and taking responsibility moved to fill in missing gaps. I learned more about how not to treat people than any graduate program could have ever influenced my outlook. Motivating others and myself became new assets. As I moved through each phase, it became obvious my why I am here changed.

The next period revolved around being a new husband and later a new father. Overlaid on those two was learning and growing into becoming a competent architect. Each of these areas had their own reasons for why I am here. As a young husband I needed to learn how to listen and communicate. I have over time been shown that to be a permanent commitment. Adapting to the role of supporting member of a lifelong union has lasting purpose. This will be looked at in detail in another letter. The same goes for becoming a father. What an awesome task, which carries both responsibilities and rewards. Growing up with love and fear out of balance produced a longer learning curve to be a better parent. Not sure how much damage I did along the way. These life experiences have influenced who I am, which in turn affects why I am here. Becoming an effective architect expanded influence both with clients and other architects in the firm. By now the why I am here is growing into more meaningful relationships and outcomes. These only increased as we founded our own firm, which will be detailed later.

Stepping back in work intensity, the why I am here changed yet again. Ultimately, I have discovered a more meaningful purpose in using experience and skills to see options for others they cannot see themselves. While it was important to know why I am here in each phase, looking back, I see a pattern of each phase building on each other to refine a more important purpose, which I believe I have come to understand. By the world's standards, just connecting dots and getting out of the way seems menial. To my understanding, the function provided is of eminent value as a part of giving people another opportunity at choice. You see, I am not responsible for the information, only a system to deliver it. The Creator provides the heavy lifting of making the connection for the person. This effort is not merit-based, just a reality of our inability to make any transformation by ourselves.

Since these letters are for you, let me give you an

example of a different point of view on an issue we have briefly discussed. I did not offer thoughts at that time as I was focused on listening. This involves the question of whether there is a Creator. This is not intended to downplay your thoughts but only provide another point of view. Further, to make this less personal, I am going to analyze an atheist's beliefs I recently heard. I am also going to use his rhetoric in reviewing his thoughts.

This man started by stating he could 100 percent prove there is no God. Most people trying to convince others do not start with absolute verbiage. The topic is difficult enough without adding more issues of doubt. I believe it was selected for attention getting. After all, this man makes his living by providing provocative statements. He stated the Bible says God is all knowing, all powerful, and all loving. His premise is, if he can disqualify any of the three or all, then that is 100 percent proof there is no God. I will not bore you with the details but will focus on the loving aspect. He questioned, how could a loving God condemn a person to eternal pain and suffering? Let us look at that question for just a minute. First, he is referring to the emotionally charged hell. It is commonly thought of as a place of torment. I have another definition to consider. For me it is just separation and rejection of the Creator. It is just an absence of relationship. It contains no hope or future. Secondly, only an all-powerful Creator would have the confidence to base all of creation on having a choice to accept or reject Him. Knowing each one's heart, He offers time and again choice with the erasing of past rejections. There is an understanding it is a process that each one will require leading and support. There is only one thing needed from us, and that is a desire to be in relationship. Lastly, given these thoughts, it is appropriate to say God condemns no one, He only memorializes your choice. You want permanent separation; He just honors your choice. If there are natural consequences to that selection, how can anyone blame God?

So from this analysis, is there another point of view to consider? Does the Creator continue to be blamed for our choices?

Following the three personal questions of who, why, and what, I believe there comes a pattern for forming direction for the future. The why I am here seems to be pivotal. It is essential to understand your gifts, skills, and experience. The who you are helps formulate the why I am here. Having direction to make decisions each day on what you are doing is dependent on why you are here.

Suggestions for consideration:

Are we just a random collection of cells without any purpose? How does knowing why I am here affect your life story?

What Am I To Do?

A sharing of thoughts and experience

Zip 121

Apel

Average Guy

Zip 121

Dear Friend,

What Am I to Do?

This is usually the first question asked each day, most often without any reference about who you are or why you are here. Therefore, we lose the benefits those observations might bring to the decisions to focus our time. Like the "why" of being here, the "what to do" is an ever-changing role. The scenario goes like this: As children, we learned what to do and what not to do. As an elementary student, we were asked to learn a musical instrument. I tried the clarinet to no avail. My unknown problem of taking verbal commands became a roadblock. The outcome is an understanding that I have no music ability. I can understand the mechanics but have no talent. I know many who do and enjoy what they can do. I am even embarrassed to clap along because I am always off.

Knowing your limits is the start of deciding what to do. In college, grades increased as classes engaged my interests and talents. I became fascinated with design and learning how to meet people's needs. This led to focusing on how to carefully build in an efficient and cost-effective manner. All facets became equally important, including detailing, codes, dimensioning, and budgets. Those were the doing of my early career.

The doing in the army experience added new dimensions to the skill set. Being able to talk openly and share thoughts publicly became a needed asset.

In addition, I learned how not to treat people. It was an education worthy of an MBA.

The architectural career was broken into two parts. I started in an office working for others to gain the missing skills. This turned into an eleven-year event. I joined a young and growing firm. Relations with clients and understanding how to interpret needs into useful designs became the focus. By the way I am wired and wanting to "prove" I am not dumb and lazy, these opportunities took on more prominence and control than they should have. My doing work took first place and learning to be a husband and new father took a backseat. This notion is exemplified shortly after our first son was born. I was assigned an almost impossible task and only two weeks to perform it. That resulted in working 192 hours in two weeks. This was not the only example, but it was the last time I did that, even after I moved on to our own firm. The point is that doing, while important, can be at cross-purposes to equally important endeavors.

The second part of the career was to open an office with a partner I had worked with for nine years at the old firm. As it turned out, we were a marriage of complementary skill sets. Our aim was to provide a meaningful service to clients needing someone to guide them. The choice in the beginning was to follow conventional wisdom and create noteworthy designs or offer measured designs that met people where they were, accepting them as is and not trying to change them. The result was a service that created its own niche. The profession followed flashy designs. While gaining some respect, we were mostly ignored and not valued by the profession. We were looked at as technically competent but lacking excitement for the future of architecture. We believed they missed the point. What we offered was content and help for the clients to achieve their goals. We had a choice and turned our back on notoriety and went on to serve twenty years as we understood it. Doing work took a shift at age fifty-five when I was introduced to the book *Halftime* by Bob Buford. It was an observation and set of guidelines to help someone move from just "doing" work to a place of meaningful impact. He told his story of his doing and transformation. It was particularly meaningful as I had been struggling off and on for three years with similar thoughts. I had worked fifty-six hours a week for twenty years and had little left to offer the firm. We had made a mistake in keeping a horizontal structure between the partners and staff for too long. We entered a transition period, which started to help the problem. The personal benefit came in as a clearer understanding of who I am and why I am here.

I came to appreciate the following:

- Talent and experience set me up to see opportunities others did not see;
- Seeing opportunities, I am to connect dots for others in need;
- This is my only function, as I am not responsible for the dots or the reaction to them; and
- I am to present the thoughts, get out of the way, and not guide the choices.

My understanding as a theist is the Creator will use the dots to offer someone more choices. This last thought revolves around my belief and trust. I have filled my role in introducing the options. It is not appropriate to force or remove free choice. This has become my current and probably final phase in doing. It also is part of the explanation for these letters.

The history shared has its purpose and meaning, but I doubt it is of much value to you, as we are all different. I do have two stories in one event that might be of greater benefit. As I understand it, most people who come to faith have some nineteen or twenty serious thoughtful encounters with acceptance or rejection of a Creator. I know I had them but have little or no recollection of them or their order. This memory occurred in 1960 when I was sixteen. I had had a few thoughts about faith and religious education but was never in a position or had the educated background to make a real commitment. I was somewhere on the path to twenty experiences but had not arrived.

I remember this event more than any sermon I have ever heard. The setting is of particular interest. I am at home watching a half-hour television show called *The Twilight Zone*. This is a secular program designed to only be provocative. What impresses me now is the Creator could lay out this opportunity, give me the choice to accept or reject it, and know the profound affect it would have in my life. For me, this reinforced the notion there is ability to do anything, use even nonreligious entertainment, know the results, and have the patience and care to deliver the opportunity. Only a Creator with power, knowledge, and love would have the confidence to offer choice.

Events that have touched me like this have created my belief system. Further, this program dealt with the consequences of our choices, just the focus of this letter. I had a decent memory of what I saw but was refreshed by going to the Internet. I would encourage you to investigate it yourself for a similar experience. The only problem is you will know the ending.

The name of the episode was "A Nice Place to Visit." The story goes like this: A small-time career criminal is shot by the police while robbing a pawn shop in his escape. He awakes with a man standing over him. He is fearful and distraught as he has never trusted anyone or strange settings. He even tries to shoot the man, to no avail. The man laughs and explains that he had been shot in the robbery and died. He went on to explain he would be his guide. He showed him to a wonderful apartment, better than any accommodation he had ever had. Gave him clothes, all the money he wanted, food and drink as requested, and three female companions to bend to his every wish. They went to casinos and won every time he placed a bet. He could not lose. He even tried using the pool table in the apartment, but in breaking the rack, each ball found a packet on the first hit. After a month of this and reviewing his own record, he decides there has been a mistake. He talks to his guide and says he does not understand why he is in heaven, and it is driving him insane, and he wants the other place.

The guide stops him and says, "What makes you think this is heaven? This is the other place," and proceeds with a sinister laugh.

The man had received all he thought would ever make him happy. He had gained without working or effort, and companionship without relationship or commitment. There was no fury or commendation, just memorializing the known hard heart and continued rejection. He had a heart issue that was not interested in fitting in with creation.

I was left to question my own motives during the last sixty years. The result is I do not always get it right, but it has helped me become a work in progress. This did not complete my education, but it was a lasting lesson. I do not have any illusions about being a complete person in this life. There is all eternity for that to happen. What is important for me is that eternity has already started. Therefore, it makes no difference where I am—I could be here, there, or anywhere. Life is moving on to what was originally intended. I am good with that thought.

Suggestions for consideration:

How does understanding your who and why affect the choices you make in life?

Do we have the ability to see unintended consequences of our choices? If so, why do you believe that statement?

Apel
Average Guy
Zip 121

Men & Women

A sharing of thoughts and experience

Zip 121

Dear Friend,

Men and Women

Since we have worked through sharing the questions, let us consider influences that have an impact on our who, why, and what. Why do you believe men and women are so different? As a theist, I believe it is to balance and support each other. There is one role difference no belief system can argue. Women can give birth to new life and men cannot. It is that simple. From that one difference all other roles flow. So if there are different roles, and if each have different requirements at different times, it makes sense to offer balance and support through one union between the two.

In my opinion, men from early recorded history have had the general roles of hunter, gatherer, and protector. As a result, for control, they have traditionally abused what they were entrusted to protect. The outcome has been a characterization of being self-centered, arrogant, and domineering. They tend to work hard, are decisive, and are more insensitive all at one time.

Women, on the other hand, because of new life, have a nurturer focus. That is a generalization and does not apply across the board. As a result of their treatment, and until recently, they appear more reserved and frustrated by the lack of equality in the partnership. In general, they are more sensitive, caring, protective, relational, and thoughtful in reasoning different points of view. Until the last half of the last century, women labored under this inequality. That has changed and is still changing. Unfortunately, the root of the problem was control and rejection of the intended order. Also, unfortunately, some of the same influences have been carried into the reform. To counter the misuse of position, women have decided to use some of the same tactics. This brings in an important consideration that has become one of my primary filters. Does the end ever justify the means? The simple answer is *no*! I could be wrong since no generalization is ever true, not even this one.

What I mean goes to the heart of the issue. As a husband, it bothers me that I am not able to share the pain of childbirth. I wish I could and have always wished that, even before our first child. It seems only right, but it is not going to change. Is it my fault? Am I to blame? *No!* How can I be a better partner? In 1970, when we started a family, we pushed to have me in the delivery room. The doctor, near retirement, had never had a father there. He did not object, as no one had ever pushed. What a life-giving event for everyone—our son, my wife, and myself. This carried on twice more and once with a grandchild. The other two grandchildren were waiting room events for obvious reasons. I could not share the pain but could offer support. This is only an example of how I understand support is intended, even if not equal. I am sure some will find fault with this analysis, but it is what I have.

Women are not receiving equal pay, which is in the process of change. When we sold the firm there were six new partners, all men. That was due mainly to the composition of the staff and prior commitments. Today the balance is three partners of each. While my partner and I do not take credit for the change, the seeds were sown for equity in all aspects of the business, both clients and employees. These examples are why people concerned with doing the right thing feel hurt and rejected when hit with the broad bush of *"all men ...."* To receive social justice, many women, not all, resort to the same control rhetoric that men used to manipulate society into their vision of control. This has become and will remain decisive. The end is correct, but the means slow the process. Hence the conclusion about the end not justifying the means. There are many men that understand and are supportive. Throwing all men under the bus is hurtful and counterproductive.

I have an analogy that demonstrates another understanding of men and women in partnership. What are illustrated here are four views of interlocking fingers and how they work together.

These figures show a man and a woman's hands in various relationships.

Figure one represents fingers loosely interlocked as in dating or early marriage. This is time when you consider making longer term commitments but are not quite there yet. Therefore, the finger contact is real but limited.

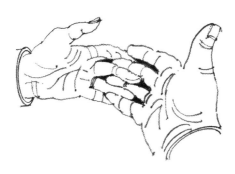

The next figure shows what happens if the relationship does not grow and become stronger. The outside forces of work, money, time, and family priorities come and attack the fragile connection. The union starts to slip apart. Hence, we have more breakups and divorce. Children become the real casualties. The loose fingers just cannot sustain the relationship.

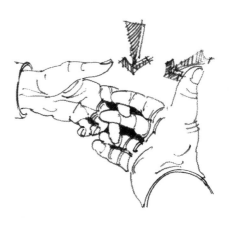

Men and women working together, over time, can become a stronger union. They can become intertwined fingers that also form a double fist. That combination becomes one that is hard to break. I believe the key to that growth comes in a commitment to support each other and learn how the other person can balance your deficiencies. This figure represents the goal we hope to accomplish.

The last figure demonstrates how the same outside forces have little effect on the union. The strands that are intertwined are hard to dislodge. The fists remain intact. Does this view not seem to be the way it was always intended to be?

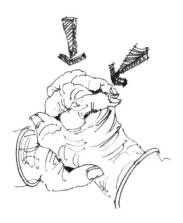

Our experience as husband and wife is not the model to follow. I would suggest, however, that time has molded us closer to figure #3, which has allowed us to see the results in figure #4. Today, neither of us would trade anything for figure #3.

This illustration is an oversimplification but seems helpful. Believing there is a plan for creation, unity needs to start with either a single person, or the union of balanced partners. Some people are gifted with more internal balance, and a union would not be helpful to live out their purpose. Marriage carried out faithfully could be an asset. Either way, creation is looking for acceptance, respect, inclusion, and support of all the different elements. This leads to the progression intended. This concept represents the focus of a Creator outside of time, space, and matter with the ability to care personally for each one.

One side issue, similar but not a part of this discussion, is consideration of the LGBTQ movement. It is appropriate that someone with a different perspective should expect to receive the same acceptance, respect, and inclusion. That would mean acceptance without judgement. I am certainly not able to judge anyone for any reason. Further, there should be equal pay, housing, and opportunity. I can give those things. What I will not give is celebration and approval. Just as there exists a right for personal belief and expression, I retain the right to stay within the understanding of my belief system. Therefore, all the equality exists, just not an endorsement so desperately desired. I did have this very discussion with someone, and it was received with grace, acceptance, and understanding. We are colleagues to this day with mutual respect. Society could benefit from this type of interaction.

Suggestions for consideration:

What would more unity and understanding of each other look like?

How would society benefit from stronger unions?

What impact would it have on the quality of your life if you understand how another might help your deficiencies?

Apel
Average Guy
Zip 121

Leadership

A sharing of thoughts and experience

Zip 121

Dear Friend,

Leadership

What does leadership look like in the who, why, and what of your life? Also, where does this skill set come from, and how is it developed? Essentially there are two groups: destructive or effective leaders. Leadership is guiding or directing a group or individual. In a world that is dominated by control and rejection, the concept has been commandeered by those that have only those goals. True leaders are few and far between. A leader can either bark out orders or try to elevate those around him or her.

When I was growing up, there were few leader examples, or I was not paying enough attention to notice. The opportunity to grow into that kind of role was limited in the 1950s and '60s. Boy Scouts was the best chance, but it was cut short by my problem with verbal instructions. I could not advance beyond second class because at that time you had to memorize Morse Code. In my case, that could never happen.

The next opportunity came during Vietnam. I had a choice to either wait to be drafted or take advanced ROTC. I choose the latter. The serious work started at basic training summer camp after my third year of college. The preparation not only included leadership but addressed many neglected areas, such as weight and conditioning. I lost thirty pounds in six weeks while eating full meals and a loaf of bread each day. I was not a momma's boy anymore.

The army is set up with enlisted ranks, non-commissioned officers, and commissioned officers. In fact, it took an act of Congress to make me an officer. All groups are separated by ranks. Noncommissioned (noncom) ranks go from private to master sergeants. Officers go from second lieutenants to general of the army. Being a second lieutenant offered the most unusual and educational place to be. You see, all the grief from the noncom side goes up to the young lieutenant, and all the incompetent grief from the top rolls down to the bottom. This year is where you learn to sort things out and determine what is important and how to proceed. This is on purpose, so the fundamentals can grow. With the task of fighting, a group needs to be unified. Two are one and one alone is none. This carries into all aspects of life. In the process, I quickly determined which officers above I could trust, and which ones did not deserve it.

In all ranks there are both good and bad, effective, and weak. I stayed away from those who were authoritarian bullies or wimps seeking to cover their position. The first are ruled by control and rejection. Their actions speak only to self-importance. The cowardly would turn on you on a dime, just to look good to someone else. Either one was dangerous, or reason to not make the service a career. It is an important lesson that they are easily spotted if you are alert.

That knowledge became a lifelong asset as it appears in all forms of relationships, especially business. After I became a practicing architect, I had a potential client tell me in the first five minutes that he was a real manipulative jerk. In a knee-jerk response, I said he was five minutes late in that admission. That should have been an insult, but he took it as a compliment. We never did work together—not out of being judgmental, but rather avoiding the stress on both of us. Sooner or later his demand for control would require doing the wrong thing for the wrong reason. Neither of us deserved that problem. So it was avoided.

There are good leaders, and that is a perspective this letter is meant to share. A real leader values other people above him or herself. While I did not serve in Vietnam, I have a feel for the real stress of conflict. A second lieutenant's typical assignment could be a forward observer, a dangerous role, to say the least. A concerned leader would send you out of necessity but never ask you to do something he or she has not already completed or would not do. Leaders use a thoughtful, considered, rational approach to giving orders. Looking out for others' well-being is the hallmark. That type of leader exacts respect and trust. This follows in living out our why in all creation.

I found those same qualities in action in a future CEO client. He could listen to an hour presentation, summarize it a few words, and list all the major concerns for him to consider. You left feeling complete in the task assigned. This is not a usual experience in the business world. You could follow him anywhere. His company was an unqualified success in many ways, not just the bottom line.

This leads to the ultimate reason for this discussion. Please follow my logic and viewpoint. If creation is made for a relationship of choice, and choice can include rejection, then wouldn't history unfold with an opportunity for everyone to reconsider their choice? By everyone, I mean all of history and the eight billion current inhabitants. Therefore, as creation was started, the Creator was rejected. History continued to unfold as planned.

In my belief system, at the right time, the Creator took on human form to lead us in another direction. Giving up power, and becoming fully human, He created an ability to relate to us that could not exist any other way. Each of the fears of death, control, relevance, attack, and future were addressed. The Creator could identify with each of the needs and had experienced them. Therefore, the offer to return to the original choice was natural. The Creator still wanted a relationship with the creation. The plan included coming in human form to lead.

Lastly, knowing rejection would continue led the Spirit to help accomplish what we cannot do ourselves. The Spirit continues the leading, but only if it is our choice. The last element is making the choice; it is not a "one and done" event. Choice is a daily need, as we are consumed with control and rejection. It is ingrained from birth and pursues us until death. Therefore, the dynamic relationship needs to be reaffirmed each day with a look to the hope and future promised. We are not expected to be perfect, only caught up in a lasting relationship. We provide the willingness, and the Creator provides the heavy lifting.

Suggestions for consideration:

What experiences have molded your thoughts on leadership?

How does leadership pertain to your living out your who, why, and what?

Apel
Average Guy
Zip 121

Discipline
A sharing of thoughts and experience
Zip 121

Dear Friend,

Discipline

Discipline is another word that spikes fear because it is misunderstood. It has a negative and positive connotation. It brings fear of punishment for poor choices. You do the crime; you do the time. That is the punishment side of discipline. These thoughts started young for all of us as we needed correction, which for many turned into fear.

The other side is the positive change that comes from inside and outside influences. These come from self-motivation, parents, teachers, spouses, colleagues, family friends, and professionals. The changes come as challenges to sport performance, time management, and any other goal-oriented challenges that need our commitment and support. While the term self-disciplined does apply to some well-motivated people, the vast majority need not only desire but outside motivation, guidance, and support to affect change. While there are disciplined people, true change rarely comes through self-determination. Lasting, constructive change comes from someone helping with the process. Further, it only occurs when the person involved wants the change. If we could do it ourselves, we would have completed it sooner.

Patience is not the same as discipline, but they appear to be close cousins. Goal-oriented, fear-driven humans seem to lack both needed attributes. Patience is willfully giving discipline a chance to provide needed change. Discipline needs time to have an effect. Therefore, leading from an outside source takes time to reach the desired level of performance.

Discipline has an impact on learning. From my experience, freehand drawing was a long-desired skill. It took several years and many failures and numerous professors and colleagues to show me the way. Over time together, we matched their experience and my latent talent and desire to create a creditable skill set to communicate design concepts. This was a sustained effort on everyone's part. I could not do it myself. Left to my own motivation, it probably would not have occurred. Discipline is kind of a mix between motivation and careful leading.

Another example is the current issue I have with weight. Given a current healing process, my body needs eighty to one hundred grams of protein each day. The unfortunate part of this is an unintended weight gain of fifteen pounds. After the requirement goes away, there will be an effort to return to a healthier weight. I will have the desire, but it will take a combined effort with my wife, family, and friends to succeed.

If we think about discipline as repetitious training, we should consider it as an option to be offered in a dynamic relationship with the Creator. As stated previously, the one with the skill set to create is outside of space, time, and matter that thinks differently. It is direction based on a value system that is different from our human understanding. Further, that interaction only occurs when both want it. Leadership and guidance happen only when both are motivated. This system is designed to be effective using our interactions with others.

Work with me here for a moment. Look at some hypothetical numbers. Let us say we have fifty interactions with other people each day. This includes spouse, family, friends, clients, colleagues, phone calls, Zoom, the UPS person, and people in the street or in traffic. No matter how slight the contact, there is interaction. Being cut off in traffic usually elicits some form of internal or external response. With eight billion people in the world, there are more than four hundred billion interactions each day. If one wanted the best for each one, there are more than enough opportunities for those to guide one or both parties in development. I see it as an opportunity to select the experiences each of us needs each day. If one has the power to create, is it difficult to assume the interactions can be arranged each day to what each person needs that day—not manipulation but leading in a disciplined way to offer better choices.

The final decision remains with us. There are still unintended consequences to be received and understood. If I were concerned for each person equally, I would benefit each equally. This would include problems and stress, if that were what was needed at the time. So, some are happy, and some are sad. It would seem the point is that each received what he or she needed at that moment. If one is stressed by an interaction, what is the cause? It could be unintended consequences of a poor choice, or you could be offering a solution to the other person that he or she needed to understand.

By unintended consequences, say you drive a car at two hundred miles per hour into a brick wall. Do you expect to survive? Death would likely be the result, and it was your choice. Given that we have free choice, do you expect the Creator to intervene in the physics? This is an absurd example. The difficulty lies in the narrow gray areas that are not as obvious. Our day is interrupted by someone with a real need, but it destroys our plans. That person needs the help, and you need to have a Creator-like heart to respond. Both have different needs, but one situation offers growth for each. Maybe this is not the day for them to receive what they want or need, but today is a start for the next time, and the next situation.

So, given the Creator's ability to understand you, who better to guide your development into the person you were created to be? As imperfect as I am each day, the ability to be motivated to seek guidance will serve myself and others. This creation is more intricate and intertwined than we can imagine. Development of who we are, why we are here, and what we are to do is available to all equally without prejudice. Our only commitment is to want to look to the Creator for guidance. No rejection from the past is considered a disqualifier. There is nothing to do to be worthy. Just a desire to fulfill the reason of why you were born. It is never too late to want to seek your purpose, only too late if you never start. While this is the shortest letter, it may be the most important.

Suggestion for consideration:

If you wanted to know your purpose, what change would it take? Would you want to be part of making that happen? How does discipline affect your desire for to have control and rejection?

What change would you want to make in you? Could you do that with the right support?

Apel
Average Guy
Zip 121

Direction
A sharing of thoughts and experience
Zip 121

Dear Friend,

Direction

Direction is a small part of discipline. It is a confidence secretly desired, which we rarely believe exists. Having a Creator be more forthright seems like hocus-pocus. It is where the label fairy tale comes into play. Once you can conceive a power not bound by worldly constraints, why is it not possible to believe guiding and leadership could come in any fashion at any time the Creator deems appropriate? We are the ones who demand communication be on our terms and ability to understand. How rude and arrogant for us to set the terms. Is it a surprise that if relationship is desired, communication is withheld until there is a sincere desire? The lack of direct communication is then used as a weapon to discredit the existence of a power beyond us. Further, when there is communication to one and not another, the label of discrimination appears, disqualifying the source. Someone who is open is just doing his or her part in receiving the information. Others refuse to accept, not understanding what is best for them. Therefore, they reject the offer. The Creator customizes the relationship and input based on understanding us and what would affect the best outcome.

In general, people struggle with belief systems because they do not understand or believe they work. For them, it just seems weird. This letter is to share the experiences I have encountered at a time I needed them the most. One entails the difficulty surrounding the decision to become a minor partner in the firm I had worked for eleven years or join someone I had worked with for nine years at the same firm. I have used this story is other places. Finding it adequate for communication, it is included verbatim. Note, this is a deviation from staying away from emotionally charged words.

A Simple Story

Friends, I am a sojourner, like you; no better or worse. I have hopes, fears, and misunderstandings. For me, the journey has been lightened by faith in Jesus Christ. I make no claims of having it all together. Just understand, in my life, He has made a difference. A relationship with Him has produced stories I believe should be shared for edification and encouragement. I have a simple story about career opportunities and decisions. This is a universal stress we all face at one time or another.

To understand the magnitude of the decision, I need to back up to the beginning of my career. In 1967, I graduated from Ohio State University in architecture. I then spent the next two years fulfilling the military obligation. During that time, I married Barb. In July 1969 we moved back to Columbus to set our roots. I started working for Trott & Bean Architects, a progressive firm. It proved a wonderful opportunity. I learned what school could not teach and had interesting clients, projects, and coworkers. I worked hard to establish myself there or for the future somewhere else. Income started at $8000/year and increased to $45,000/year by 1980. I considered making a permanent place there, going out on my own, or partnering with someone else during those eleven years, never losing sight of the future or the next step.

Now comes the story. I am going to include a day-by-day account so you understand the sequence and pressures. After much pushing from me, Dick and Jim offered an opportunity to buy a minor share of Trott & Bean on Monday before Memorial Day in May 1980. It would take borrowing $40,000 at 3/4 percent over prime, which was 21 percent. I could be fired at any time, and they would repay the value at 8 1/2 percent over ten years. My income was not tied to my performance or their income. I had to trust they would be fair, which they had been.

The next day I received a call from Dennis Meacham inquiring about working together. Denny was three years older and started work at Trott & Bean three months before me. Denny had been a minor partner, but it did not work for him. He started his own firm two years earlier. I told him I was considering an offer from the firm. He said we should at least have lunch to talk about it. So, on Thursday, we set up a time to review the possibilities. During that hour, we decided we could work together, and there was probably enough work to start. I would buy in by paying a sliding scale of any extra money earned. Accounting in a small firm required taking money at the end of the year to avoid double taxation. I would pay 80 percent the first year, then 60, to 40, to 20 percent, to even. The difficult part was taking a $5000 cut in pay, back to $40,000/year. Barb and I had just had our third child in April. The most important part in discussing working together that day was explain to each other the things each did that drove the other one insane.

So now the stage is set for the big decision. I had Friday, Saturday, Sunday, and Monday to decide. Come Tuesday, Dick, Jim, and Denny needed to know what I was going to do. I had told Dick and Jim about considering going with Denny. I spent Friday and Saturday weighing all the pluses and minuses. By Saturday night I had completely beaten the subject up. I knew all I was ever going to know and was no closer to an answer. On Sunday afternoon I was just praying. In the quiet I heard a voice in my head ask a question. I took it to be Jesus asking which one I would choose if either would be right in my life. I thought for a minute and answered: I would probably go with Denny because I would have more direct accountability with the clients. Working at Trott & Bean, my responses to clients were always filtered by Dick and Jim's values since I was representing them. I would be freer to give my opinion directly to the client. So, He said He would guarantee that either one would be right in my life, but I would still have to choose. The conversation helped me understand I was asking the wrong question. Once I understood the heart of the decision, it became clear what to do. Notice, He did not say make you financially successful. He said make it right in your life. Later that came to mean getting a job two hours before we were going to lay off our first two employees, and learning to take responsibility for our mistakes and to defend ourselves when not at fault.

Meacham and Apel was started with a promise: "To make it right in your life." This brings me to the purpose of telling this story. There comes a question only you can answer whether you were involved in the firm or observing now. If we are loved equally by God, if we understand there is no special consideration to me, then is it remotely possible to "make it right in your life" extended to clients, employees, consultants, and contractors?

This question is worth contemplating.

This is a story I have told many times. It is a valuable part of my growth and understanding of a dynamic relationship with the Creator. At thirty-five, when this event happened, I was relatively young in my belief system. Growing as a husband, father, and young architect, faith never received the attention it should have.

There are two main points of focus for this letter. First, a positive answer to "making it right in my life" is a demonstration of how the interrelations work that are part of the Creator's options. As I saw it, a client could receive designs more suited to its needs. Employees could develop in a place to make a career. Contractors could operate in a fair system. This is a dynamic relationship that addresses each one fairly and equally. We were not perfect at it, but the possibility existed when it had not before the new firm. Second, if you think about the event, no tables were levitated, no ghosts, no weird unexplainable happenings, just a minor leading into the correct question. I was so tied up in trying to figure out what to do, I had skipped why I was here. This is one of the sources for the belief that we do not consider the questions in the right order. Once I understood the error, the decision became history.

Direction and leading play a major role in helping us live the full life we were intended. Helping in this case did not remove choice. I still had to choose. What if I had stayed with the old firm? How would it have been right? Good question, as the firm suffered illness and broken relationships in a few years. I have never looked back and do not intend to start. It does not take too much to believe either the outcome would have changed for each person there with input, or I would have been able to pick up the pieces. The point is moot, but having confidence of things working out was not in doubt. While the new effort was not promised success, and rolling economies put things on edge, the firm grew from three to thirty-five employees in the next twenty years.

There is another example of being given direction that involved giving. Our church was in a giving exercise to buy land for a future campus. It was several months in consideration and discussion. We had as a family evolved into tithing over time. This effort would be over and above the tithe for three years. It was a difficult decision, as giving seemed maxed and we were about to enter the college tuition era not well prepared. We were looking at three kids over a ten-year span. Two would overlap in the third and fourth years. The problem was we had only managed to save for one child for one year. Given our circumstances, we decided on an amount to pledge. On the day to commit, in the seven-minute drive to church, I was led to believe that number was wrong. It was to be increased by fifty percent. We did not flinch, just added it in trust.

Fast forward to the third child's graduation, and on that day all three educations had been paid without residual debt. This happened not because we had it figured out but because of trust. Things happened along the way we could not have known or counted to happen, such as the county buying part of our frontage for road widening. The result was continued giving and matched needs. This type of leading produces less stress and more focus on true issues of concern.

Another example is being given a solution to a problem eight years before the need. As an architect, I had an interest in more effective and functional housing. While studying various issues, I was led to a solution I called the directed lifestyle. I have always seen this as an answer to some of our self-inflicted problems as a society. Basically, it allows someone to expand and contract in the same location over his or her lifetime. It involves two connected units, one small and one larger. There is a schedule of moving back and forth in the units. One could save twenty-five percent in cost and energy over your span. I wrote a seventy-page book to explain the pluses and minuses. The true value comes in the choices available as there are life changes. I have not been able to develop these ideas due to a lack of resources or interested partners. I have tested the concept on a countless number of people with positive results. We as a family were able to use it to help reestablish our single-mom daughter in her own home. It has worked well for both her family and ours. It is intergenerational living that supports each other. Again, openness and trust produced less stressful solutions with answers better than we could image.

There is one other different example that adds to our contemplation. This is about obtaining clarity and the value in understanding who you are. I have talked about positive direction received, but there are also negative parts that are important. So there are positive and negative attributes that affect our quality of life. The most glaring one in my life: I am not a reader. I have determined many reasons for that, but they are not important here. I am envious of those people like my wife who consume books weekly. I would like to be drawn into that world. Change in this instance has not produced the desired result. What do I do with this information? In this case, I accept who I am and find ways to compensate. The result is more focus on the positive traits I do have. This has helped my understanding of why I am here and what I am to do. Beating myself up for who I am not, is a fool's errand.

Suggestions for consideration:

What direction would be fulfilling in your life journey?

Are we in a frame of mind to accept direction?

Apel
Average Guy
Zip 121

Pain
A sharing of thoughts and experience
Zip 121

Dear Friend,

Pain

Pain is one of the most universally avoided experiences we face. In a divisive world, the desire for avoidance has common ground. We see pain as mental, emotional, or physical in nature. Examples of mental could be Alzheimer's or autism. Emotional could be parent or caregiver to the same groups. Physical could include all forms of cancer, disease, the aging process and many other aches and pains.. The question for contemplation: Does pain ever provide anything positive to the quality of life?

Before we proceed, I believe there are some basics that need attention. Part of these letters have focused on belief in a Creator. Many in disbelief cannot wrap their minds around a Creator who would allow pain in any form. That view denies the very makeup and self-description of the Creator. If the desire is the best for us, then we assume pain would not be included in our life journey. What is not considered is the matter of choice. Some, not all, of what is thought to be pain is simply the natural consequence of rejection of the Creator. We demonstrate a lack of love for Him, self, and others which defies the Creator's intention. The problem lies with not having or caring to have a relationship with one complete enough to create us. Promising complete choice and not interfering with the results of rejection, we have chosen pain over belief and trust. So, driving a car at a hundred miles per hour into a concrete wall ends in a painful death. This is an over-simplification to make a point. It was a choice, so why apply the results to the Creator?

Further, a similar question is, "Why do bad things happen to good people"? Again, it is a faulty question, as I believe no one is good. All fall short of what we were intended to be in this creation. There may be moments of doing the right thing for the right reason, but that is often short-lived. We are dominated by a desire for control and rejection. I know this from living my own life. Belief is not a one-and-done concept. It can be daily, sometimes minute by minute to recommit. We are so fixated, and incapable of self-help, that only the care provided by the Creator and the Spirit can make a difference. This example extends to the concept of love. If one takes any human definition of love and peels back to the essence, you will find that of a caring Creator. The care, concern, feeling, emotion, and intensity only comes from the Creator. Love has been plagiarized and perverted by humans for their own purposes, not the genuine article we attempt to control.

Given that perspective along with the concept that there exists a value system we cannot comprehend, the Creator ultimately plans on the best for each of eight billion people each day. The point is that pain is the result of poor choices, or it is permitted for an ultimate outcome that is better. We only see pain in the short term. The Creator has a longer view and determines which is the best all-around solution. We also have no desire to give the authority to the One who rightfully deserves it. One who creates has the right to make those kinds of determinations. Who are we to limit such power?

In summary, pain is the currency that buys hope and understanding that the world cannot offer. Pain can yield a benefit to the quality of life that is unobtainable any other way. In the end, pain may just be the best for us and those around us. As this view points out, it is not always about us. The big picture includes others affected by the experience and what is best for them.

Now, going back to the examples of pain, either experienced or witnessed, I know firsthand the effects of living with Alzheimer's disease. Mother and Grandmother died after a long stint of suffering from mental decline. It robs one of dignity and self-worth, leaving no quality of life. As researched as it is, the answers remain to be found. Causes and solutions are still awaiting discovery. Grandmother's history was an education not sought. Nursing homes were just that, homes with unskilled staff to warehouse the dying. That started my mother's demand to never by put in a home like that, ever, period! This later had ramifications as my brother, and I waited too long to act when she needed help. Between Grandmother's death and my mother's decline, the forecast robbed my mother of life to the fullest.

My understanding is life is found in the present, not in the past or future. Coming from the stern parental mold, Mother did not fully share her faith perspective. While I cannot know, the evidence would indicate that fear of prolonged disorientation outweighed peace and joy that family and other activities could have provided. Now I face the same questions she had after her mother's death. Will this someday be my fate? I have the same choice to make, but mine was altered by watching her. Through the grace shown in seeing life missed, I have been given a different direction. I am not consumed by the possibilities but simply accept the possibility exists. Much can happen and change before that hour comes, if ever. I believe and trust, and that settles it. Her pain became my unmerited gift. Further, this gift has been passed to others around her and my children. In this case, pain provided learning that was priceless.

Autism provides yet another look at the effects of pain. Pain comes to a person in not knowing what the day will bring. It is a mental anguish not asked for nor sought. For parents and caregivers, it is equally heartbreaking to live a life pattern without a positive future. One effort has focused on creating a sustainable, safe, predictable lifestyle that gives the opportunity for a full quality of life. Talking to the parents, you receive a combination of messages. Yes, the unpredictable is hard and frustrating to plan out and live. They are limited in options for their own lives, which need rest and positive reinforcement. Many marriages do not survive. There is little going out to dinner, and almost no vacations. With this input, all you can see are lives mired in pain. How does this happen and why? We do not know. Some believe this is the result of environmental factors, diet, or medical treatment. In that case, it could be a consequence for poor society choices. Have we chosen chemicals that cause those issues? Was there time and care given to insure complete study of affects? The answers have not been found even though there has been a large effort and many studies. At the very least, the results indicate some outside influence exists to cause the sudden influx of occurrence. . Unfortunately, this adds to the list of unanswered questions.

On the positive side, listening to some long-term surviving parents, you get a different than expected perspective. These people have experienced the gift of this person. They passionately believe everyone has a purpose, including their child. Their ache is for others failing to see and know that purpose. Therefore, the person with autism has purpose, the parents have grown through the pain, and the world waits to learn about the beautiful soul they are missing. Somehow, I see a positive side to this awful burden. What if the only way to appreciate your life is to experience others' pain? I cannot explain it, but it seems possible. This approach is not human by nature. But that does not mean it does not exist or is not of value. I wish you could listen and experience the love and care expressed by these parents. They are easier to find with the increase of occurrence. It was once 1 child in every one hundred and fifty., now it is one in fifty-five. Most people I know have family or a friend with a child with autism. Just ask, they are there waiting for someone to care. It inspires me, and I believe it would spill over to you.

The next example is of physical pain, just plain discomfort rated one through ten. I have watched the experience of the effects of cancer over the years. I have come alongside and walked with many. I want to introduce you to Charlie. I met him seven years into his ten-year battle with a rare form of leukemia. I only wish I had met him sooner to have a more complete picture of his life. The short time I had with him gave me plenty of inspiration. Charlie was general counsel for a large insurance company. I am left to image what a thoughtful, determined opponent he must have been. The time of his illness was spent like many patients', with ups and downs, chemo, and remission. The last couple of years were spent on a liquid diet carried in a bag with a tube in his side. We met most weeks on Monday night in a men's group at Church.

Charlie, through his experience, developed into an incredibly strong man. Be sure, he had feet of clay and would share that with you. He, however, had developed a spirit that would not let him down, no matter the pain. He became the epitome of belief and trust. Yes, there were frustrations and days of anger, but he never let that have control or damage his faith. He was a consistent inspiration and learning tool to each of twenty-some men. But the influence went way beyond us. At his funeral, six hundred people felt and left with the same kind of life-changing inspiration. Part of that came from listening to each of his children talk about his influence in their lives. Charlie was a great example, not of his own doing. The Creator cared more for him and the people around him. Ultimately, we were the beneficiaries of Charlie's life purpose through pain.

So far I have shared the examples of others. How have those influenced my life? Everyone has some form of pain or trouble. It is said we progress through three states: just leaving, struggling, or just about to enter. It is part of the life experience. Most problems are human-made in struggling with the fears of death, relevance, control, attack, and the future. In many ways I have had relatively few opportunities to be tested. For me, belief and trust have grown over time to be a salve to self-inflicted destruction.

I have an example in my own life of a broken relationship. Usually there comes understanding of the reason for the lost connection, but not in this case. I have neither an explanation, a cause, or the ability to fix it. It is like a disease with no known cause or cure. Through the experiences shared, I have come to a place of acceptance, as I see the possibility of a greater good. It is either for my growth, the other person's, or probably both. While living with this is hard, I refuse to let it rob the present. At some point in this life or the next, it will be made whole again. That is the trust end of the bargain.

Lastly, the idea of a patient Creator having all the time to wait for acceptance leaves out the positive everyday effort provided to move creation forward. The Creator is still at work and not absent to be just a watcher. Many, for their own control, would like us to believe there is no active plan. This idea dismisses the refining that takes place every day in each of our lives. Like heat applied to molten gold, the dross can be skimmed off with the power of pain. I find it an effort and right that is not accountable to human judgment. All His efforts include a fact we overlook, that the Creator also suffers pain. We experience parenting pain with our children's rejection. How much greater is the pain of being rejected by eight billion people every day? We understand there is this pain as it is written that, in fact, He wept.

I have concluded pain is the currency that provides faith, understanding, and trust that nothing else can, and that's the point.

Suggestions for consideration:

How have you experienced a positive result of pain?

If you have not seen the positive, what might it look like in your life?

Value Of Life

A sharing of thoughts and experience

Zip 121

Apel

Average Guy

Zip 121

Dear Friend,

Value of Life

The value of life becomes an inherent part of us, like DNA. Each of us has our own take on what that means, and it is part of who we are. How it is developed or nurtured separates us from other parts of creation. Predator animals accept feeding on others as natural. We, on the other hand, are more subtle. We lose the value of another person when control and rejection dominate. We do not necessarily physically destroy but often do worse with verbal abuse.

The value we place on others can be on an individual or a group. I can feel a strong connection to another person. The contact back and forth expresses appreciation and respect. This develops into a desire for more with a closer connection to the goal.

In my case, the first example was that of my nuclear family. It was made up of Mom and Dad, who were Depression-era driven as they married two months before the 1929 Great Depression. They were not even able to live together the first years and were separated by thirty miles during the week. I also had two brothers, one twelve years older and the other eight years older. I have come to understand the profound impact this had on developing who I am. Each added something different. Dad, being an engineer, devoted much of his time and skills helping friends develop creative solutions for their problems. Mom was a constant, even too much of a nurturer, who had lunch ready when I walked home at noon from elementary school. It was not the lunch but being there and listening.

The eldest brother showed a steady work ethic while laboring under stress to perform as the first child. Expectations were piled on him as they learned their parental roles. This left him to endure a system of trial and error.

The second brother was the original rebel without a cause. As a part of that, he also was the funniest person I have ever met. He could find something to poke at in any situation.

These details are important because each lived out his purpose by influencing who I am. My perspective is to accept, appreciate, and celebrate each one in the nuclear family. They have all parted from this life and no longer provide continued influence. I do not make an idol of those memories but find a healthy balance as I remember their investment in me.

Dad died forty-six years ago, David left forty-two years ago, and Jack left twenty-seven years ago. Mom was last at twenty-four years ago. As would naturally be expected, focus has shifted to my wife and family. For me, I celebrate but do not idolize my initial family.

What I take away from the first family to give to the second is love and heart. I see the issue is learning to discern the essence of heart, how one develops the ability to offer complete acceptance and love. I believe the struggle goes beyond control and rejection. I have spent years learning what heart is and what defines it is a lifelong event. We do not have just a belief problem; there is a lack of ability to comprehend the magnitude of the

Creator's heart for His work in creation. I expect to spend this life and the next getting just a basic understanding of the intention to all people, creatures, and aspects of this world. The point is, we have a heart issue, not just unbelief.

Before I leave the nuclear family, there is one story of grace and care by the Creator for my brother David. In his rebellious state he ran away to get married as he finished undergraduate work and was ready to start veterinary medicine. In the mid-1950s this became a family tragedy. My parents spent three days and nights crying over the past and fearful of the future. Being only twelve, I was sent upstairs and excluded from all discussion.

Fast forward twenty-three years. David had gotten married, had three children, got divorced, and was remarried and living in Vancouver. Then I was thirty-five, a husband for eleven years, father of two, and young in my faith journey. As part of a new awareness, I attended a weekend retreat, which was a powerful milestone. After that event, I left with a clear intention to write Dave a letter to share growing feelings and regret being shut out in his time of trial. It seemed like a positive move to share and grow together again. It was a new invitation, like these letters. There were no motives or expectations. I could only offer choice, but it is up to others to accept or reject. Over the years, communication was sparse and lacked depth. I knew of no problems, had not judged, and had no means to have an opinion. I just knew I was being encouraged and wanted to share. To not seem to be focused on him like a judgmental rant, it was written to all three, mother and both brothers. I am including it here, verbatim, as it has a powerful point about the

Creator's love and care. Note this letter includes many of the emotionally charged words I have tried to avoid. But they are necessary to make the point.

Sunday, March 25, 1979

Dear Mom, Jack, and Dave,

Surprise! A letter from your son and brother. This is a special time and place, set aside to tell each of you my feelings. It is, in fact, a love letter.

Jack, I love you. I enjoy the relationship we have. You are someone I look up to and admire. Diligence and consistency are characteristics marked in your work at the electric company and at home as father and husband. In my life, I will be eternally grateful to you for being God's instrument to keep me in church in the early 1960s, when it did not seem important.

Dave, I love you, but that cannot be apparent from my actions. I hope you can forgive me for not writing or making the effort to go see you these last eighteen years. It is this failing that is partial inspiration of this letter, but the love is true. Our blood relationship was cemented in growing up together in a strong family. Memories and experiences we shared cannot be eased with time. It is a wonderful feeling knowing that even though we are apart, we are always ready to accept each other, no matter what we have or haven't done.

Mom, I love you as only a child can love his mother. I know my brothers join me in this love and appreciation. The things we accomplish in our work or in our families are because of you and Dad, with a lot of help from God. We are sorry that you do not receive the time, care, and concern you deserve from us. Your gift to us is so large, and we do not know how to thank you. Nothing we can humanly do can repay the years. I would suggest the only token we can offer is to pass the same love, concern, time, money, and years on to our children, your grandchildren.

Now that you have heard my feelings, I want to share even more with you about why this letter is sent to you. This love letter and the real inspiration is Jesus Christ. He thinks it is important for you to know that I love you, but even more important is that He loves you, each one of you. He wants, in a new way, for you to dare to believe the Bible. Believe that Creation is a world with choice, living and working in personal relationship with God. Believe that through choice, man has, with sin, tried to destroy the relationship. Believe God has never taken choice from us. Believe that God wants that personal relationship, not through fear but love—love enough to become a man, to die for us, and to show us the way to a personal relationship.

What is this personal relationship? Simply, God wants to meet us all our needs here in this life and cannot do it without communication. He wants to be a physical active being in your life and wants it to grow each day of this life. We know so little, and He has so much for you and me.

How does it work? God has many channels, but there appear to be three main areas: daily study of the Bible, fellowship with other believers, and constant prayer in which He literally speak to your heart, if you let Him.

Jack, I know of your long-term commitment to Jesus Christ, but you cannot out-give Him. He has more help and aid for you in the pressures of your work. Your weight loss is an example of His care for your health, as I am sure He was involved. He has many new opportunities at Upper Arlington Lutheran. Please consider marriage encounter, Cursillo, and others as opportunities to grow closer to the Lord each day.

Dave, I know that in many ways life has been a struggle, but not until right now could I tell you that it does not have to be. Jesus Christ wants to help David Apel every day of his life. Dave, I do not know your real feelings, and it is not important that I know them. If you have not made a real commitment, or would like to renew your confirmation, I would ask that you read what you can, look for a fellowship, and ask Jesus's help, for He will show you the way. Even if you think He is not real, ask Him in. Tell him to show you and He will. If you have made that commitment already, then you will know why I urgently write this way. I pray that your new work and marriage can be forged together with a personal relationship with Jesus Christ. This should offer a fulfilled and peaceful life.

Mom, I know the loneliness and physical pain must be impossible burdens, but His promises are just as rich and true for you. I pray for the relieving of your pains. I would hope you would seek a closer fellowship at either Holy Trinity or Upper Arlington. I also hope you will be freer to tell us your needs and use us, for we are His instruments for carrying out His promises. Also, I have one last hope for you—that you would understand that we all fall short and do not merit His love or favor. Please come back to the communion table to receive the full measure of grace Christ has for each one of us.

Now, this letter may seem to be too much! Please bear with me, for I have one more request. Please put this letter away for a few days and then reread it.

In the second reading, try to replace me with Jesus Christ. He wrote this love letter to each of you, just as surely as you are reading it. Let Christ speak to you of love.

I am only human and therefore no better or worse than you. Please accept this letter with all the love that was intended. If Jesus Christ and the story are not true, then I am a fool, and this letter is a joke. But the fact is He is real, and the personal proof to you is in the feelings that you are experiencing right now, and in our love for one another. I plan to spend the rest of my life growing in this relationship with Jesus Christ; won't you please come with me and do this as a family?

Love, Bob

This letter is only the start of love and care. The rest of the story lies in the troubles Dave was experiencing. You see, six weeks later, David took his own life at forty-three. There are important lessons for everyone here.

First, the Creator used the letter to reach out and accept Dave even though He knew what he was about to do. I see rejection is in two forms. One is stubborn independent control. The other is a set of things that happen or are done to someone. I do not have the position, skill set, or authority to make judgments. This gets added to the list of things I do not know or understand but one day will.

Second, the letter was used to relieve me of years

of guilt I could have had. The Creator looked out and provided for each of us when neither understood the need. That is the type of care I have never experienced anywhere else.

Value of life extends to care for actual life, not killing to be exact. Part of choosing military service was to complete school without interruption. Architecture school was five years. ROTC was four years with an automatic deferment of one year to complete school. By the last year, I had completed four years of ROTC and six weeks of summer camp/basic training. I had learned war did not make sense but was a reality. WWII was probably one of the few that appeared to be legitimate as there was a true threat to world peace from three tyrannies. Vietnam, on the other hand, seemed more like a political maneuver, which as time went on became a polarizing national issue.

The original choice of ROTC was based on limited adult thinking and consideration. At the time, my belief system was nominal at best. To my surprise I struggled for the deferred year as to whether to accept the commission. This was done without any political motivation. It was more focused on the consideration of value of a life. Could I kill another person? As a side issue, was the fear attached to kill or be killed? Second to those, were the responsibilities afforded a leadership role? The concern was not the stress of anti-war or the religious call to do right. It was just about how to value another human. It revolved around that love essence I call my heart. If heart was not committed for the right reasons, I would be a bigger detriment than an asset. People like that end up being fragged (deliberately injured or killed). I was not concerned with why I am here, just what to do. That reflected my maturity level. Without seeing a bigger picture that I was intended to be part of, I looked for a way to make sense out of the decision. This was the first time I used an analogy. I saw the taking the commission like anteing up at a poker table. In poker, to play there must be a pot to start, which comes from the ante. How could I take the benefits or share in the fruits of a free country if I could not even put in the commitment? A simple analysis took almost a year to come to mind. The final answer prioritized the lives of fellow soldiers: two are one and one is none. It put in perspective the responsibility as a citizen, keeping in mind the political and military decisions made were not in my control or skill set. I still had value for the combatant, but that would be decided in the field.

Today, I do not feel I can share the honor rightfully given to those that had to face kill or be killed.

Abortion is a critical consideration of the value of life, but I concluded years ago, society had taken a pass on caring. The arguments are divisive, callous, and designed to shed responsibility. In my simple brain, it is not rocket science. Abortion is murdering a defenseless unborn child, period! This is just my opinion, which I believe you are entitled to know. It is too complex an issue for these letters. I come at the discussion from two directions. One, I believe it is wrong. Two, the issue deserves thoughtful input as there are many issues unresolved that people can bring the love and grace of the Creator. Women should have more respect, care and support for the difficult birthing task assigned. There should be more education and support for contraception. Lastly adoption should be made easier, supported, and encouraged. Saying no is not the answer. Saying we can do this together will be a start.

People say it is a right. Really? Who made it a right and by what authority? If the defenseless can go, am I next as an older person who may need medical care? Who gets to decide? I am told my perspective is not valid since I cannot give birth and do not experience the pain. Guess what? Without men, there is no discussion. Procreation is designed to have attraction for each person. The attraction soon displaces the implicit responsibility that comes with the possibility of new life. We satisfy ourselves and reject the results. We feel we are entitled to one without accepting the responsibility. Abortion is just a way to shed the commitment to a new child that would require a lifetime of love and care. The design is you cannot have gratification without responsibility. Humans desiring what they want, when they want it, have manipulated the system. I have no problem with contraception, which is preventing procreation until the responsibility can be included. But even those methods are not always affective. In those cases, responsibility should be honored.

Most abortions are for birth control and medical reasons. Even the medical reasons can be dubious. Case in point is our energetic eleven-year-old granddaughter. Early in the pregnancy, it was discovered she would have a severe birth defect. Her parents did not elect abortion based on faith and trust, not fear. She survived, and it took five years and insurance support to make her a healthy child with an adult future. Currently, she plans to be a veterinarian. What would the world have lost without belief and trust?

I recently read a similar story not related to abortion, but it makes the same point about how we do not always understand the interconnections. A doctor helped a mother deliver a premature baby. He spent the next sixteen hours struggling to save the child, which was successful. Fast forward thirty years to a car accident that left the doctor hanging in a burning car. The EMT who rescued him was the boy he had saved. How has society robbed itself of such interconnections and service?

Similarly, the Creator is accused of permitting pain, such as cancer. How could that be allowed to continue? The cure for cancer exists; we have not yet discovered it. So the question back is how many of those aborted were given the gifts and passion to make that discovery and were killed? Whose choice was that? Control and rejection strike again, not making any sense.

Given who I am, I find acceptance of people and change to be normal. I am pliable in many cases, but not abortion. I reject it for the following:

- Killing a defenseless fetus is wrong.
- It denies the Creator's legitimate authority.
- It denies the child's purpose.
- It denies the world of that purpose.
- It potentially harms the participants.

I have found a degree of peace in knowing there are few values that are not negotiable. I accept the fact society has made this legal and I am in the minority. The concern is for this callous disregard and the unintended consequences.

Suggestions for consideration:

In your life journey, how do you value life?

What ways might you change or help others place more value on people?

Right & Wrong

A sharing of thoughts and experience

Zip 121

Apel

Average Guy

Zip 121

Dear Friend,

Right and Wrong

There are as many answers to that analysis as there are people. Over time, I have developed six bullet points addressing the question of right and wrong, broken into two categories.

- The first is indignant right, which could not be wrong and has no proof. The person knows it all and knows all he or she ever will.
- The second is right with modest acceptance and some proof to hold that belief. They consider themselves just plain right.
- The third is on the fence and might be right. They are wrong but just hoping someone will agree.

The last three pertain to being wrong.

- The first is maybe wrong. They know they are wrong and just want to bluff someone.
- The next is wrong. They know it and accept it. There is hope for these people as there is an understanding some correction is needed.
- The last one is no way wrong. This person has blinders on how others perceive their actions. Like indignant right, there is little hope for successful resolution to any problem.

As an architect, much of my time was spent working out miscommunications. The construction process has three main players, which provides many opportunities for issues that need resolution.

1. The owner often has little to no experience with the process and needs more explanation and a reason to trust the process.
2. The contractor operates at a deficit in the previous discussions that set the budget, aesthetics, and priorities. They are often not at the table when decisions are made. Many times, they must rely on the information from the drawing and specifications.
3. Lastly, the architect is challenged to represent the owner's needs to the contractor.

Given the possible combinations of misunderstandings, I found time and effort were needed to keep projects moving forward in a positive direction. The goal was not the building but keeping a positive construction experience. Every project built with everyone having positive reinforcement turns out with better quality. I have no data to prove that statement, but I know it is true. Therefore, I had to develop a problem-solving technique. I called it what do I know, what don't I know, and what would I like to know.

In the simplest of cases, one of the three participants made a modest mistake. This is more easily resolved in that one takes responsibility and moves forward. This is a rare occurrence as I find there is usually some right and some wrong in each of the three. Having a little right spurs defense. Defense leads to slow down and hard feelings. With the approach I used, the focus was on determining the severity of the problem and need for change.

Thus, what are the givens? Provided there are no substantive issues of health, safety, or welfare, does the issue need change? Is it aesthetic? Can the owner accept it and live with it? Why would that ever be considered?

First, I have never worked on a perfect project. People naturally make mistakes all the way around the process. Why should someone benefit when mistakes are made? Corrections should be made, but enrichment of the project should not be part of the solution. The solution should not include free materials and labor if they were always needed. Occasionally, people try to cut corners hoping for acceptance. That is a different story, which soon becomes apparent. That motivation requires change.

Second, living with a minor flaw keeps the contractor engaged in a positive way, usually appreciating the grace and more watchful to the end of the project. So, arbitrary insistence or measured response—which one serves the client best? Further, I believe this concept so much, on occasion, we took responsibility in gray areas to move the project along a positive vein. It served the client better than a time-consuming fight. If the issue had some error on our part, it only made sense to put the time and money into the solution instead of defense. It also turned out the client and contractor were more open to understanding their part and more open to participating.

The final solution method was name "Right, wrong, and what are you really going to do?" As I mentored others toward the end of my active career, I tried to promote this philosophy, to little avail. It seems control and rejection know no bounds. This view of problem-solving did not appear overnight or come as a way out of trouble. It simply came as a reaction to trying to understand all sides. This course of action was frequently met with scorn or rejection, often from my own side. It was perceived as weakness, and foolish. I tend to give everyone the benefit of their position, with the understanding it will be returned. It is a working form of treating others as you would like to be treated. If consideration is not returned faithfully, there are then other actions to be considered with valid reasons.

The conclusion I have come to believe is that being right is not the most important criteria. The driver coming home at night who is killed by a drunk driver is an example. He is totally in the right but is unfortunately dead. Therefore, your position may be correct, but accepting some responsibility may be the wiser choice. Hence the name "Right, wrong, and what are you really going to do?"

The interesting thing about the six reactions to right and wrong is that most of us engage in at least one every day. Taking responsibility for our actions directly hits our fears of control, death, relevance, attack, and future. We are consumed by it because it touches all fear nerves. Fearing all sorts of consequences both real and imaged tends to distort the truth, which has become an endangered value. I am not sure truth was ever given its rightful place in the human experience. Since each of us engage in these practices, it becomes easier to say no one is "good," not even one. The only exception to that thought was the Creator coming in fully human form—human in form but not subject to rejecting the Creator.

The term sin is applied to everyone but difficult when thinking of newborn babies, or mentally affirmed. Babies seem to get up to speed quickly. I believe a simple definition of sin is rejection of the Creator. The word sin is emotionally charged as it represents all sorts of control issues. It is seen as breaking arbitrary human rules or laws. While some of that is true, it is the desire for control that rejects the Creator. Our actions are only a manifestation of that rejection and denial of the legitimate authority of the Creator.

Suggestions for consideration:

How has your view of right and wrong affected your life?

What changes to your perspective could enhance your journey?

Apel
Average Guy
Zip 121

Disunity
A sharing of thoughts and experience
Zip 121

Dear Friend,

Disunity

The essence of control in others is keeping people disunified. Conflict throughout history echoes this reality. Humans are the crowning touch in creation. They were always meant to live in unity and oneness with the Creator, and each other. Choice left the door open to separation, which came early in history. From there it has been perpetuated everyday by everyone.

These letters were started two weeks before the latest attention getting events of the pandemic, and civil unrest. Both of such magnitude and in that order to grab the even most uninterested into full attention. I cannot remember such events or sequence. I was led to start this project as an invitation to another perspective by sharing my life experiences. The emphasis was to offer that perspective to those hurt by modern day Pharisees. Therefore, it seemed appropriate to avoid emotional charged words. Words that caused hurt and misdirection. I believe that was correct in the first letters, but I am convinced the last two letters must be clear, concise, and open. These thoughts require transparency. Remember, convincing anyone is outside my skill set and responsibility. I only stand to offer another opportunity for choice. Only God the Father, His human form, Jesus, and their Spirit can exercise those functions. I can only offer my experience. Their job is to do the heavy lifting. They have the power, authority, and opportunity to fill in the voids of understanding and belief. The need for this effort has existed from the beginning with the rejection in the garden.

Starting with my experience, I can testify to the love and care afforded in my development. I have alluded to it before, that parents and outside influences can do things to us. How do we make people responsible for things done to them? Hard to explain, but we do it every day.

I grew up in a house that was stained with prejudice. My parents did not just dislike, but hated Catholics, Jews, Blacks, and Unions. Each night I would hear about one group or on big nights all four. It took many years and avenues for me to reject those messages and learn to seek the heart of God to return to what life was intended. It took exposure to other people to learn the truth. It took a helpmate to come along side to show the way. I did not make the transformation, Jesus did. I was only open to the mountain of evidence of erroneous thinking. My wife was a social worker that performed redeterminations for aid to dependent children. Society helped to enable the fatherless home. Aid only given to fatherless homes. Today it is common to decry the absent father that the system created. How do we hold people accountable for unintended consequences?

After rejecting prejudice, which required years, I came to grips with understanding and accepting my part, and understanding my parents, just as they were. They too had development issues that skewed them. Being first generation Americans and starting married life in the depression, caused plenty of opportunities for them to feel oppressed and develop prejudice. The point here is history has a way of keeping the fires of disunity engaged.

But God has a way to work with each one of us if will just yield. I did not deserve the change, but the world did. The creation was intended to be unified. The transformation does not rank us perfect, just a work in progress.

Disunity has been spurred by the ever-deteriorating political climate, both here and around the world. It is disheartening to see everything reduced to lies and manipulation from all sides. People my age remember more cooperative times. The common good outweighed special interest. Some want to return to the "good old days". Problem is they never existed. The underlaying hate and mistrust were always there, just not as public. Believing things were better is a fantasy. To that poor memory we have added the need for instant results and gratification. Speed takes difficult relationships and puts another unsustainable layer to cause more problems.

Currently, there is loss of income, disruption of the whole economy, loss of work, loss of freedom, frustrations from discrimination, and fear of public lawlessness. Does this summary miss anything from the instant grief currently experienced? Many have multiple solutions. Many have been tried and failed, but we going to try them again. As Einstein said, insanity is trying the same thing over and over and expecting different results. Most of those ideas are aimed at getting back to a pseudo peace. They are band-aids to get back to being comfortable and ignoring real change. Fortunately, or unfortunately, I believe the magnitude and complexity of current issues will not allow that course of action.

I hope, and believe, these events were allowed to happen to offer the world another chance to reset to the original intent, which included unity. God works everyday in everyone to provide transformation. The change I received prevented my children from being exposed to the hatred I experienced.

Coming back to the intended path has rewards rarely discussed or appreciated. Getting closer to God's will, including unity, is where peace and completeness are found. The world does not and cannot offer either. Having alignment in unity with each other will remove many of the fears that drive us. Being a brother or sister with each other removes fear of death or attack. Having a plan and goals for each to live in hope removes fear of the future and relevance. Lastly, feeling under control is a natural outcome of unity. Feeling comfortable requires less manipulation of others. While the current stresses give us magnified fears, I see hope in the opportunity for global transformation.

While this Pollyanna like dream seems improbable, I go back to not underestimating the will, skill, authority and love of God the Father, Son, and Spirit. Humans can deny all they want, but that does not lessen Their resolve or ability to prevail. As stated before, peel back the layers and you will find God is the definition and essence of love. Humans did not invent it and cannot sustain it. All these issues are heart issues. We are not looking to align our hearts and efforts with God. He provides the strength, guidance, promises, and hope. All these issues have come into focus quickly but were centuries in the making. Remember, I believe God is outside of time, space, and matter. Therefore, time is not a concern. Take whatever time is needed. Make whatever physical changes in matter or space to bring about unity.

This will be a long process. To start, society needs realistic expectations. I do not expect resolution in my lifetime. Fifty years might be a good start. God can make it happen sooner but that might be at the expense of choice, which He will not do. Pain will be an ingredient to change. It is a part that produces perseverance, which in turn produces character, and character produces hope. Hope does not disappoint. These are guarantees given by God, as He loves us more than we love ourselves. Originating and sustaining love, He understands in ways we are not capable of obtaining. Each one of us must examine the condition of our heart alignment. Understand the deficiency in not being the same that God intended. Starting with ourselves will open the opportunities to share that heart attitude with others. It will be adopted by faithful presentation of sincere change, not jawboning oratory.

Everyone, including myself, wants to know what to do next. There are many options and some not so good. The basis for change is to understand who I am, and why I think I am here. As I see both sides of issues, I need to learn and understand more than the superficial reality I have of the experience of discrimination. What does it really look and feel like. The other side equally needs to understand the limitations and frustrations I experience as an old white, American, male. No group is more despised, hated, and distrusted. Many pains were started before me, and I have such limited control to influence real change. It is impossible to repair the past. Efforts should be made to correct the future. Seeing the need for change, and being dismissed, controlled, and manipulated, leaves one ineffective. There is pressure for correction but without any stature.

Given that outlook I have proceeded by forming a new relationship with another man from a weekly study. Kevin has the discrimination, and I am the old white guy. As we get to know each other there will be a productive open sharing that should allow the helpful information exchange. The common goal each have is God given transformation. That work will be facilitated by learning from each other. He can share the fears, frustrations, and pain. I can share the fears, frustrations, and pain of being part of a system I inherited. I did not invent it. I have benefitted from it but have no real interest in sustaining it. But I am told that offer is not enough. Throwing money at problems without accountability is a failed attempt from the past, doomed to fail again. Money cannot solve misplaced heart issues.

As Kevin and I move forward, I see an analogy. It is like we are on a two-thousand-mile journey, and we are only into the first two hundred feet. We are walking a dirt path which will lead to sidewalks, which will lead to side streets, which leads to collectors, which lead to main thorough fares, which lead to interstates. Each new level will add other people making the same trip. Together we will all move in the same direction with new understanding and unity. Given my age, I do not expect to make it to the side streets or thoroughfares. The complete trip will extend beyond my allotted time. As I am not there, others we have met along the way will fill the void. This is God's work and timing. The world would do well to heed the invitation.

Another thought is the now common desire to eliminate racism. Overnight it has become more universal. The current call seems to dismiss the progress made. Granted it is not as consistent and down to the level of every person, but progress has been made. I would suggest a good start to adding speedy change would be to stop talking about it. Keeping the focus on black and white seem counter to eliminating color as a description. Physical descriptions ignore the issues. Let us work on eliminating fear and adding hope. A person should not fear to be in public and profiled with evil intent. They hope to go to the store without being hassled. Another person should not fear protecting life and property being characterized as extremist. They hope to have the right to protect themselves and family. Casting doubts on people without evidence is destructive. This type of character doubt is applied to men, and women, rich, and poor, young, and old, citizens, and immigrants. Correcting injustice should eliminate issues nonsense and focus on people wanting complete control over others at all costs. Therefore, the focus needs to be on discernment of criminal intent over self-serving promotion.

The process will be long and painful but rewarding. Further, especially at my age, I expect the process to continue into the next phase of life after this one. I fully expect and look forward to learning and finding new understandings that I currently lack. I do not have the ability or capacity to understand the complexity of life. When I am ready, it will come. This view gives hope for a continued dynamic relationship with the one that created me in the first place.

Suggestions for consideration:

What heart attitudes are you missing that would bring your life closer to god's intention?

How can you make a difference in the process of reconciliation?

How can you help bring a new alignment?

Apel
Average Guy
Zip 121

Finishing Strong

A sharing of thoughts and experience

Zip 121

Dear Friend,

Finish Strong

I have previously stated the following, but it is included for emphasis as this was the genius for the desire. The idea to finish what one starts has been with me most of my life. About eighteen or nineteen years into Meacham and Apel Architects, I became restless and confused about the future. One of the old fears of life. We had developed and brought along many others in their careers. The office had grown from the original three to thirty-five employees. In hindsight, we kept the organization to horizontal and had not given others the responsibility they needed to grow. The lack of client responsibility prevented a healthy office development. The partners had worked fifty-six hours a week for all those years. I was beginning to doubt what else I had to offer the firm. This continued for two years until I was introduced to a book called *Halftime*.

The author, Bob Buford, wrote about his similar experience. He discovered that when some of the early money issues of children and family need changing, it was time to go back into the locker room of life and discover what more meaningful things one could do. He did not tell you what to do but how to figure it out. He figured out how to help pastors become better managers.

This led to a discussion with Denny about selling the firm to the next generation. I was fifty-six at the time. Over the next year we worked with six potential new partners. They would receive control, and we would continue to work for the firm on salary and receive differed compensation over the next ten years. This allowed a smoother transition, with us remaining to work with longtime clients. Each partner had a different skill set. We believe the firm had the best chance of success if they brought those skills. They had the opportunity for increased success if they focused on their skills. Eventually, two did not understand or share the same vision. When asked if we failed, my answer is no. It was up to each to make it work. It was their responsibility, not ours.

Over the ten years as we stepped back, I found new opportunities to use experience and skills to benefit others. That was Buford's whole point. Not everyone could do what he did, but they could do something for others. I found it. The first major project was a kids camp in Honduras. It provided camp experiences for four thousand city kids per year. It had the best soccer field in Honduras. It was complete with a covered outdoor gym, dining hall, water and sewer facilities, and cabins. Raising funds and slow construction required ten years to build. The size of camping ramped up over time. A ministry with few resources and plenty of volunteers was able to come to true fruition. This became the start of many pro bono projects. It has often been either I help, or no one helps. I am okay with that as I see this work as a natural extension of my who, why, and what. It also developed an acceptance of a humbling support role and not out-front leader.

This experience and others have led my "semi-retirement" into continuing to be as busy as I have ever been. While I do work for a fee, most is guided by simple need. Why in the world should I waste the experiences, mistakes, problem-solving and architectural skills when there are so many groups with limited options? The result over the second ten years has been a new awareness of the importance of what I now understand as my who, why, and what. The point is the more I am open to needs and having a minor role, the more I am living out what I was intended to be. That feeling, which is fleeting and rare, is indescribable; I am not able to put it into words either of us could understand. There is a peace and completeness that escapes words and feelings. To put it into world terms, a trillion dollars would not even be a down payment. Did I deserve these feelings and experiences? No, I was just open to an invitation. God had plans for my skills and people who needed them. You know God works hard. My offering belief and trust was repaid in ways I never imagined. Past rejections were not held against me. All that was wanted was a simple desire to join the word and heart of Creation. For me it is like finding a cure for cancer, why would I ever keep it to myself. I do not imply I have the answers, just suggesting your needs and responses are different. God meets everyone with custom-tailored solutions if you just ask. I am only an example of what God, Jesus, and the Spirit can do. Trust me, your answers will not look like mine as you are a different who, why, and what.

There is one last analogy. Let us say life is a series of auto races. Along the way you have driven many different cars with varying degrees of success. Cars have been old, worn, unreliable, high maintenance, and slower than others. You always performed as well as you could with what you had. You now realize there are only a few opportunities left to win. You have an opportunity to race a top performer but have always been reluctant to try. You understand it outperforms all others, comes with its own crew, does not run out of energy, and is your best chance. You shy away because you do not believe the claims, or the front people have hurt you in pushing.

Here is an offer for a test drive with two requirements. First, it is a test drive to see if what you heard is true. The wrinkle is you only get to ride, not drive. The owner's son does all the driving until you are ready. The second requirement is you must want what is being offered. You need to want to sign up. Past performance is not a factor. Once you buy into the program, your commitment to hard work and worldly abuse is all that is required. Everything else is covered by the owner of the team. This is a standing offer issued to all those interested in finishing strong.

Well, these letters have offered one person's experiences and views. Just an average guy, nothing special. In summary, one last thought. Belief and trust in many cases have overcome control and rejection. I still find I fail as much as I succeed. The point is I am forgiven, live in grace, and am supported by the team of Father, Son, and Spirit. The result is undeserved love, joy, peace, patience, kindness, goodness, and self-control. I fully expect to receive rejection and scorn from all sides. We are not promised smooth sailing. We know it will be the opposite. I am okay with that arrangement. The army taught me I could put up with anything for a short time.

Whatever waits can only have a short day. For you see, all the fears that rule us have a new answer. Eternity has already started, so death is reduced to a time of transition. Attacks have an affect only if not prepared, and trust is assurance enough. Control is better left for God, Son, and Spirit, who have absolute authority. Relevance comes from finding heart in the Creation. The future goes on and on. It does not stop with death. I have work and learning to be continued.

Last Question:

This is an invitation, as shared in these letters. Will you consider it, reconsider it, or reject it?

The Supporting Word from God

Once you have made it through all the letters and have an interest in more understanding of my Christian experience, I offer these themes from scripture that have come to me over several years. I have not found the development of faith to be one and done or come with great speed. We all take a long time to process what should be more natural. Further, we are impeded by our default setting of wanting to maintain control and rejection. In the end, I have come to embrace belief and trust.

All the letters share themes in one form or another from God's Word in the Bible. This summary is not exhaustive or the complete resource. The whole Bible is.

The first one goes to establishing the answer to, "Is there a God?" I have come to that conclusion by starting with the first words of the first verse.

> "In the beginning God created the heavens and the earth" (Genesis 1:1).

This shows God is outside of time. He was there at the start or the beginning. He created heaven, which is space. He created earth, which is matter in the space. These three thoughts make a case in my mind for a God who not only created but loves and sustains all who joyfully give themselves to a lasting relationship with God, Son, and Spirit, which are the various forms presented to all mankind. No matter the background, everyone has the evidence of creation all around them, all the time. Knowledge and the invitation are part of being in creation. The key factor in the invitation is choice. God knowingly give humankind free choice to accept or reject Him. This was part of the plan for two reasons. He did not want mindless robots or forced subjects. Further, He wanted to demonstrate His love for each creature. God does not intervene with dramatic results because that would remove free will and be a manipulation. Our rejection comes with natural, predicable consequences that are most often allowed. Again, preventing them would take away choice. The image of God in three forms comes later in Genesis 1 along with a blessing and direction for the purpose and function of male and female.

> Then God said, "Let us make mankind in our image, in our likeness, so that they will rule over the fish in the sea and the birds in the sky, over the livestock and all wild animals, and over all the creatures that move along the ground." So, God created mankind in his own image, in the image of God he created them; male and female he created them. God blessed them and said to them, "Be fruitful and increase in number; fill the earth and subdue it. Rule over the fish in the sea and the birds in the sky and over every living creature that moves on the ground." (Genesis 1:26–28)

The start says "let us," indicating all three forms were there from the beginning. God understood humankind would reject Him. The Son and Spirit were not plan B and C. God therefore operates on a dimensional level and value system we are not capable of understanding as there is no earthly human experience to compare and form judgments. This also explains allowing pain and suffering as they can have a positive outcome for the person in His value system. Better short-term pain for long term gain. Not being subject to time pressures, as humans are, His short-term time frame can be intolerable to us. These verses also give humans responsibility to multiply on and subdue the earth. This command is for males and females equally. As usual, what the directions are and what we do are drastically different based on a desire to manipulate and control. This is where control and rejection start.

This leads to the concept of each of us having a purpose. The verses in Jeremiah tell of mankind's rebellion, which leads to exile. After seventy years, restoration will come. These verses are meant for them but are an example of the love, care, and concern shown to His creation.

"For I know the plans I have for you," declares the Lord, "plans to prosper you and not harm you, plans to give you hope and a future. Then you will call on me and come and pray to me, and I will listen to you" (Jeremiah 29:11–13).

While not directly referencing us, this is a demonstration that all life has purpose and is to have hope if God is included.

The rest of the Old Testament is history of mankind's development and thirst for control and rejection. It includes stories of a reset with Noah, and prophets, kings, and warriors, a violent history setting up the second phase of creation. The quality of life was fixed and determined for self-destruction as it could not get its hands around the offer for relationship with the Creator. In the proper time, God came humbly as a servant in the form of a man, Jesus Christ. His life was short at thirty-three years and of that, only three years of ministry. The offer was reconciliation to enable the original offer. The task was to offer a new start for mankind to be able to have a relationship with God. It entailed giving direction and consult and offering forgiveness for God rejection. The ministry was laid out as forceful instruction but most often in a gentle way.

This thought is captured in the woman at the well. We see this in John 4.

> Now he had to go through Samaria. So, he came to a town in Samaria called Sychar, near the plot of ground Jacob had given to his son Joseph. Jacob's well was there, and Jesus, tired as he was from the journey, sat down by the well. It was about noon.
>
> When a Samaritan woman came to draw water, Jesus said to her," Will you give me a drink?" (His disciples had gone into the town to buy food.)
>
> The Samaritan woman said to him, "You are a Jew and I am a Samaritan woman. How can you ask me for a drink?" (For Jew do not associate with Samaritans.)
>
> Jesus answered her, "If you knew the gift of God and who it is that asks you for

a drink. You would have asked him, and he would have given you living water."

"Sir," the woman said, "you have nothing to draw with and the well is deep. Where can you get this living water? Are you greater than our father Jacob, who gave us the well and drank from it himself, as did also his sons and livestock?"

Jesus answered, "Everyone who drinks this water will be thirsty again, but whoever drinks the water I give them will never thirst. Indeed, the water I give them will become in them a spring of water welling up to eternal life."

The woman said to him, "Sir, give me this water so that I won't get thirsty and have to keep coming here to draw water."

He told her, "Go call your husband and come back."

I have no husband," she replied.

Jesus said to her, "You are right when you say you have no husband. The fact is, you have had five husbands, and the man you now have is not your husband. What you have said is quite true."

"Sir," the woman said, "I can see that you are a prophet. Our ancestors worshipped on this mountain, but you Jews claim that the place where we must worship is in Jerusalem."

"Woman, Jesus replied, "believe me, the time is coming when you will worship the Father neither on this mountain nor in Jerusalem. You Samaritans worship what you do not know, we worship what we do know, for salvation is from the Jews. Yet a time is coming and has now come when the true worshippers will worship the Father in the Spirit and in truth, for they are the kind of worshippers the Father seeks. God is spirit, and his and his worshippers must worship in the Spirit and in truth."

The woman said, "I know that Messiah" (called Christ) "is coming. When he comes, he will explain everything to us."

Then Jesus declared, "I, the one speaking to you—I am he." (John 4:4–26)

This story illustrates the ability to lead a person through the consequences of poor choices without a lecture and destroying self-worth. Coming at that time of day, she had lost all esteem and was shunned by other women. He spoke a gentle word to help her understand she could be redeemed and have another chance. What she had was not working well for her. Jesus was kind but offered scorn to the Pharisees that should have known better but were married to power and control. While He did not condone the lifestyle, He offered another way. I believe this is our lesson to receive from her story.

Jesus continued to cement His place in showing another way, pointing to true reliable concepts, offering forgiveness and payment for our rejections. No other entity has offered to show the love it takes to die for another's transgressions. God knew how history would enfold and the price to demonstrate the commitment to His creation. This is summed up in my favorite meaningful verse, John 14:6: "Jesus answered, 'I am the way and the truth and the life. No one comes to the father except through me. If you really know me, you will know my father as well. From now on, you do know him and have seen him.'"

In this one verse is a summary of His time with us. The offer of another reset with God. This points to what I believe is not an issue of living right or wrong. It is rather living in an honest committed relationship with one that loves us more than we love ourselves. He is not here to push or demand. The true problem is a heart issue. Can we find the heart of God and align ourselves with him? When our hearts become so hard as to not ever turnback, then we take on self-chosen separation, which humans call condemnation. God does not condemn us; we choose to separate ourselves. Separation comes bringing unintended consequences. The angst we fear and want to avoid comes to make a home in our lives.

God knowing what is needed does not stop with coming in human form. He knows that is an important piece but not all that is needed. Jesus told His followers that is was better for Him to leave so that the Spirit could come and minister to them with knowledge and power. Just before the ascension, Jesus lays out the plan.

> He told them, "This is what is written: The Messiah will suffer and rise from the dead on the third day, and repentance for the forgiveness of sins will be preached in his name to all nations, beginning at

Jerusalem. You are witnesses of these things. I am going to send you what my father has promised: but stay in the city until you have been clothed with power from on high." (Luke 24:46–49)

The power is that of the Holy Spirit. He is the original third part of the plan from the beginning of time. God would walk and talk with His creation in the garden until rejected. He worked through the law, prophets, kings, and all forms of human rejection to only move to the next phase of coming as a man as Jesus. He offered a return to relationship without penalty but was rejected and crucified. He took the next planned step and defeated death on the third day. Before He ascended to the Father, He commanded to wait for the Spirit.

We live in the same time frame, which has lasted two thousand years. With all this, we are determined to call it a fairy tale because it threatens control. Belief and trust come to us to help solve our heart issues. The Spirit of God supports and comes alongside us to give us the promises of creation. We now have the opportunity to live as children of God and become the people God always intended us to be.

The practical application of the Spirit is summed up here:.

But the fruit of the Spirit is love, joy, peace, forbearance, kindness, goodness, faithfulness, gentleness, and self-control. Against such things there is no law. Those who belong to Christ Jesus have crucified the flesh with its passions and desires. Since we live by the Spirit, let us keep in step with the Spirit. Let us not become conceited, provoking and envying each other. (Galatians 5:22–26)

Which of these nine attributes—love, joy, peace, forbearance, kindness, goodness, faithfulness, gentleness, and self-control—does anyone not desire to fill in their lives? I personally can testify that in my original state, none of these were possible. God's plan was complete but to date is not finished. Obtaining any close facsimile of these traits would enhance the quality of anyone's life. Unfortunately, they are not one-and-done propositions. Even having the plan presented, and being in the phase of the Spirit, we all, including myself, slip back into rejecting God every day. Everyone is a work in progress. None of us ever achieves perfection in this life.

In the future, I am looking forward to the next phase where I will start to learn just what I do not know. I will have the topics but not the answers. I will have an eternity to learn the intricacies of God's creation. For me, eternity has already started. It makes no difference where I am or when. I can live out my purpose here or learn to be the person I was intended to be. The world as we know it cannot and will never be able to offer this kind of peace.

To be clear, this is not a panacea view. Included is the realization that there will be pain and suffering. What is different is they will come with a purpose. I can live with that view. Nowhere is there a promise to remove turmoil; in fact, they are realistically promised. Life in believing and trusting comes with those challenges, or trust would not be needed. I fully expect to be rejected for the thoughts in these letters. Either they do not fit someone's narrative or are a threat to their worldview. Neither side has proof of their position, which is why both require faith.

My view is based on reinforcement I have received over a long period of time. I have received in some measure each of the nine traits. The Spirit has worked to develop them, not because I am special or deserve them. I have peace I would not trade, and rejection for sharing my thoughts will not be able to snatch it away.

These thoughts are reinforced in verses in James, which summarize the logical extension of belief and trust.

> Consider it pure joy, my brothers, and sisters, whenever you face trials of many kinds, because you know that the testing of your faith produces perseverance. Let perseverance finish its work so that you may be mature and complete, not lacking anything. If any of you lacks wisdom, you should freely ask God, who gives generously to all without finding fault, and it will be given to you. But when you ask, you must believe and not doubt, because the one who doubts is like a wave of the sea, blown and tossed by the wind. That person should not expect to receive anything from the Lord. Such a person is double-minded and unstable in all they do. (James 1:2-8)

I can testify that perseverance has had a positive effect on issues I have faced. The result is an undeserved confidence that pain or solution both will have a lasting impact on the quality of life. More than teaching by others, God has used these experiences to reinforce His promises in my life.

From where I am now, God's plan of coming as Father, Son, and Spirit has given me an honest picture of who I am, why I am here, and what I am to do. I am not perfect and have no expectations of being able to present that picture. I see life as an ongoing work and partnership with the One who created me. The bottom line is to live life in belief and trust.

One Last Thought

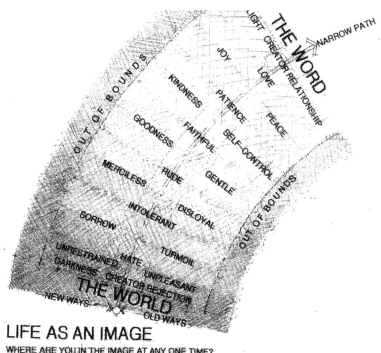

LIFE AS AN IMAGE

WHERE ARE YOU IN THE IMAGE AT ANY ONE TIME?
WHERE ARE THOSE AROUND YOU IN THE IMAGE AT ANY ONE TIME?

THE DIFFERENCE BETWEEN THE WORLD AND WORD IS ONE "L" OF A DIFFERENCE

The focus of these letters is about being offered another chance at choice. We have that everyday whether accept or not. This image is helpful for me to maintain focus. We can continue to embrace the attributes of darkness or choose to move toward the attributes of light. We know three things about the journey. First, we will not reach the full light in this life, that is the purpose of eternity. Second, being human beings, we are going to move constantly within the image. This is not a constant path. We need to understand and accept that is our nature. Third, trying to ignore by running out of bounds is not a solution as the same darkness is there. We need to take old and new ways of thinking to forge a narrow path to the light. We do also understand the quality of life increases as we are able to focus on moving toward the light. I find this the purpose of the image. May you find it useful to remind you of where you and those around you are moment by moment.